Communication & literacy. Loving communities to overcome race, class & gender inequalities (read, write & think critically) are crucial to healthy communities & relationships that are not marred by race, class or gender inequalities.

teaching
Community

White supremacist capitalist patriarchy.

Xenophobia — unreasonable fear of strangers

Nationalist imperialism
think Vietnam: Imperialism, leads to nationalism
Insurrection — rising in revolt

hegemony
Leadership or predominant influence over another

Critical consciousness — perceive social, political & economic oppression & take action.

Pluralism — Recognition and affirmation of diverse
Distinct ethnic, religious or cultural groups are
present & tolerated in a society

sexual iconography

misogyny

Teaching
Community

A Pedagogy
of Hope

bell hooks

Routledge
New York and London

Published in 2003 by
Routledge
29 West 35th Street
New York, NY 10001
www.routledge-ny.com

Published in Great Britain by
Routledge
11 New Fetter Lane
London EC4P 4EE
www.routledge.co.uk

Routledge is an imprint of the Taylor & Francis Group.

Printed in the United States of America on acid free paper.

10 9 8 7 6 5 4 3 2 1

An earlier version of "Teaching 13: Spirituality in Education" appeared in
The Heart of Learning, edited by Stephen Glazer (Jeremy Tarcher/Putnam:
New York, 1999).

Cataloging-in-Publication Data is available from the Library of Congress.

ISBN 0–415–96817–8 (hb)
ISBN 0–415–96818–6 (pb)

It is imperative that we maintain hope even when the harshness of reality may suggest the opposite.

—Paulo Freire

Contents

Preface

Teaching and Living in Hope

Ten years ago I begin writing a collection of essays on teaching—the end result was *Teaching to Transgress: Education as the
Practice of Freedom.* In the early stages of discussing this project
with my beloved white male editor Bill Germano, many questions were raised about the possible audience for this book.
Was there really an audience of teachers and students wanting
to engage the discussions about difference and struggle in the
classroom that were the core of this text? Would college professors want to read this work? Were the topics broad enough?
I was confident then that there were many educators out there
who, like myself, wanted to engage in a dialogue about all
these issues. Once the questions were answered we forged
ahead with publication. Immediate response from readers let
the publishers know that the work was timely, that its conver-
sational tone made it an easy read, offering readers an opportunity to return to chapters, work with ideas they found new,

difficult, disturbing or just plain ideas that they disagreed with and wanted to think through. More than any other book I have written, *Teaching to Transgress* has reached the diverse audiences I imagined would be its readers. Bridging the gap between public school teachers and those of us who do most if not all of our teaching at colleges and universities, these essays focused on common issues teachers confront irrespective of the type of classroom we work in.

Certainly it was the publication of *Teaching to Transgress* that created a space where I was dialoguing more and more with teachers and students in public schools, talking with teachers training to be teachers, listening to them talk to me about teaching. The incredible success of *Teaching to Transgress* motivated my editor to urge me to write another book on teaching shortly after the publication of this first book. I was adamant that I would not write another book about teaching unless I felt that sense of organic necessity that often drives me to passionate writing.

In these past ten years I have spent more time teaching teachers and students about teaching than I have spent in the usual English Department, Feminist Studies, or African-American Studies classroom. It was not simply the power of *Teaching to Transgress* that opened up these new spaces for dialogue. It was also that as I went out into the public world I endeavored to bring as a teacher, passion, skill, and absolute grace to the art of teaching: It was clear to audiences that I practiced what I preached. That union of theory and praxis was a dynamic example for teachers seeking practical wisdom. I do not mean to be immodest in openly evaluating the quality of my teaching and writing about teaching, my intent is to bear witness so as to challenge the prevailing notion that it is simply too difficult to make connections—this is not so. Those of us who want to make connections who want to cross boundaries, do. I want all passionate teachers to revel in a job well done to inspire students training to be teachers.

There are certainly moments in the classroom where I do not excel in the art of teaching. However, it is crucial that we challenge any feeling of shame or embarrassment that teachers who do their job well might be tempted to indulge when praising ourselves or being praised by others for excellent teaching. For when we hide our light we collude in the overall cultural devaluation of our teaching vocation. A big basketball fan, I often tell audiences, "Do you really think Michael Jordan does not know that he is an incredible ball player? That throughout his career he has been gifted with a level of skill and magnificence which sets him apart?" *And there are days when he does not play well.*

In the past ten years I have spent many hours teaching away from the normal college classroom. Publishing children's books, I have spent more time than I ever thought I would teaching and talking with children, especially children between the ages of three and six. This teaching takes place in various settings—churches, bookstores, homes where folks gather, and in diverse classrooms in public schools and at colleges and universities. The most exciting aspect of teaching outside conventional structures and/or college classrooms has been sharing the theory we write in academia with non-academic audiences and, most importantly, seeing their hunger to learn new ways of knowing, their desire to use this knowledge in meaningful ways to enrich their daily lives.

When I first began writing feminist theory, always talking through ideas with other feminist thinkers, one of our primary concerns was not to collude with the formation of a new elite group of women, those college-educated women who would benefit the most from feminist thinking and practice. We believed then and now that the most important measure of the success of feminist movement would be the extent to which the feminist thinking and practice that was transforming our consciousness and our lives would have the same impact on ordinary folks. With this political hope we made commitments to seek to write theory that would speak directly to an inclusive audience. With the academization of feminism, the loss of a mass-based political movement, this agenda was difficult to achieve in a work setting where writing acceptable theory for promotion and tenure often meant using inaccessible language and/or academic jargon. Many amazing feminist ideas never reach an audience outside the academic world because the work is simply not accessible. Ironically, this often happens in those fields like sociology and psychology where the subject matter is organically linked with choices people make in everyday life. One example concerns feminist work on parenting, particularly writing on the value of male parenting. Yet much of this work is written in arcane academic jargon. Even dense books, which are not terribly full of jargon, are hard for tired working people to plough through, selecting the parts that could contain meaningful material.

As my academic career advanced, my yearning to take my intellectual work and find forums where the practical wisdom it contained could be shared across class, race, etc., intensified. I have written theory that many people outside the academy find difficult to read, but what they do understand often compels them to work with the difficulties. Concurrently, I have completed a body of popular writing that speaks to many different people at the level of their diverse learning skills. Not only do I find this exciting, it affirms that the mass-based goals of feminist politics that many of us hold can be realized. Indeed, we can do work that can be shared with everyone. And this work can serve to expand all our communities of resistance so that they are not just composed of college teachers, students, or well-educated politicos.

In recent years mass media have told the public that feminist movement did not work, that affirmative action was a mistake, that combined with cultural studies all alternative programs and departments are failing to educate students. To counter these public narratives it is vital that we challenge all this misinformation. That challenge cannot be simply to call attention to the fact that it is false; we also must give an honest and thorough account of the constructive interventions that have occurred as a consequence of all our efforts to create justice in education. We must highlight all the positive, life-transforming rewards that have been the outcome of collective efforts to change our society, especially education, so that it is not a site for the enactment of domination in any form.

We need mass-based political movements calling citizens of this nation to uphold democracy and the rights of everyone to be educated, and to work on behalf of ending domination in all its forms—to work for justice, changing our educational system so that schooling is not the site where students are indoctrinated to support imperialist white-supremacist capitalist patriarchy or any ideology, but rather where they learn to open their minds, to engage in rigorous study and to think critically. Those of us who have worked both as teachers and students to transform academia so that the classroom is not a site where domination (on the basis of race, class, gender, nationality, sexual preference, religion) is perpetuated have witnessed positive evolutions in thought and actions. We have witnessed widespread interrogation of white supremacy, race-based colonialism, and sexism xenophobia.

An incredible body of texts has emerged that stands as the concrete documentation that individual scholars have dared, not only to revise work that once was biased, but have courageously created new work to help us all understand better the ways diverse systems of domination operate both independently and interdependently to perpetuate and uphold exploitation and oppression. By making the personal political, many individuals have experienced major transformations in thought that have led to changing their lives: the white people who worked to become anti-racist, the men who worked to challenge sexism and patriarchy, heterosexists who begin to truly champion sexual freedom. There have been many quiet moments of incredible shifts in thought and action that are radical and revolutionary. To honor and value these moments rightly we must name them even as we continue rigorous critique. Both exercises in recognition, naming the problem but also fully and deeply articulating what we do that works to address and resolve issues, are needed to generate anew and inspire a spirit of ongoing resistance. When we only name the problem, when we state complaint without a constructive focus on resolution, we take away hope. In this way critique can become merely an expression of profound cynicism, which then works to sustain dominator culture.

In the last twenty years, educators who have dared to study and learn new ways of thinking and teaching so that the work we do does not reinforce systems of domination, of imperialism, racism, sexism or class elitism have created a pedagogy of hope. Speaking of the necessity to cultivate hope, Brazilian educator Paulo Freire reminds us: "The struggle for hope means the denunciation, in no uncertain terms of all abuses . . . As we denounce them, we awaken in others and ourselves the need, and also the taste, for hope." Hopefulness empowers us to continue our work for justice even as the forces of injustice may gain greater power for a time. As teachers we enter the classroom with hope. Freire contends: "Whatever the perspective through which we appreciate authentic educational practice—its process implies hope."

My hope emerges from those places of struggle where I witness individuals positively transforming their lives and the world around them. Educating is always a vocation rooted in hopefulness. As teachers we believe that learning is possible, that nothing can keep an open mind from seeking after knowledge and finding a way to know. In *The Outrageous Pursuit of Hope: Prophetic Dreams for the Twenty-First Century* Mary Grey reminds us that we live by hope. She declares: "Hope stretches the limits of what is possible. It is linked with that basic trust in life without which we could not get from one day to the next . . . To live by hope is to believe that it is worth taking the next step: that our actions, our families, and cultures and society have meaning, are worth living and dying for. Living in hope says to us, 'There is a way out,' even from the most dangerous and desperate situations . . ." One of the dangers we face in our educational systems is the loss of a feeling of community, not just the loss of closeness among those with whom we work and with our students, but also the loss of a feeling of connection and closeness with the world beyond the academy.

Progressive education, education as the practice of freedom, enables us to confront feelings of loss and restore our sense of connection. It teaches us how to create community. In this book I identify much that stands in the way of connectedness even as I identify all the work we do that builds and sustains community. *Teaching Community: A Pedagogy of Hope* offers practical wisdom about what we do and can continue to do to make the classroom a place that is life-sustaining and mind-expanding, a place of liberating mutuality where teacher and student together work in partnership. Whether writing about love and justice, about white people who transform their lives so they are fundamentally anti-racist at the core of their being, or about the issue of sex and power between teachers and students, or the way we can use the knowledge of death and dying to strengthen our learning process, these pages are meant to stand as a testament of hope. In them I work to recover our collective awareness of the spirit of community that is always present when we are truly teaching and learning.

This book does not belong to me alone. It is the culmination of many hours spent talking with comrades, students, colleagues, strangers. It is the outcome of life-transforming dialogues that take place in the context of community-building. Vietnamese Buddhist monk Thich Nhat Hanh teaches: "In a true dialogue, both sides are willing to change. We have to appreciate that truth can be received from outside of—not only within—our own group . . . We have to believe that by engaging in dialogue with another person, we have the possibility of making a change within ourselves, that we can become deeper." Openly and honestly talking about the ways we work for change and are changed in these essays, I hope to illuminate the space of the possible where we can work to sustain our hope and create community with justice as the core foundation.

Parker Palmer believes that enlightened teaching evokes and invites community. Many of us know this is so because we teach and live within the life-enhancing vibrancy of diverse communities of resistance. They are the source of our hope, the place where our passion to connect and to learn is constantly fulfilled. Palmer states: "This community goes far beyond our face-to-face relationship with each other as human beings. In education especially, this community connects us with the . . . 'great things' of the world, and with 'the grace of great things.'. . . We are in community with all of these great things, and great teaching is about knowing that community, feeling that community, sensing that community, and then drawing your students into it." Hopefully, *Teaching Community* will draw you in and renew your spirit.

Teach 1

The Will to Learn

The World as Classroom

When contemporary progressive educators all around the nation challenged the way institutionalized systems of domination (race, sex, nationalist imperialism) have, since the origin of public education, used schooling to reinforce dominator values, a pedagogical revolution began in college classrooms. Exposing the covert conservative political underpinnings shaping the content of material in the classroom, as well as the way in which ideologies of domination informed the ways thinkers teach and act in the classroom, opened a space where educators could begin to take seriously what it would look like to teach from a standpoint aimed at liberating the minds of our students rather than indoctrinating them. Imperialist white-supremacist capitalist patriarchal values were taught in the all-black schools of my Southern childhood even as those values were at times critiqued. In those days black teachers who were themselves usually light-skinned (since those were the individ-

1

uals the color caste hierarchy allowed to be upwardly mobile and receive higher education) definitely showed favoritism, giving respect and regard to fairer students thus reinscribing white-supremacist thought, even though they might also teach that white enslavement of black people was cruel and unjust, praising anti-racist rebellion and resistance.

In this space where they offered alternative ways of thinking, a student could engage in the insurrection of subjugated knowledge. Hence it was possible to learn liberating ideas in a context that was established to socialize us to accept domination, to accept one's place within race, sex, hierarchy. Of course, this same practice has been true in all forms of schooling. As women, mostly white, entered schools and colleges for the first time, learning from the patriarchy, their very presence was itself a moment of insurrection, a challenge. Within in the patriarchal academy, women have consistently learned how to choose between the sexist biases in knowledge that reinscribe domination based on gender or the forms of knowledge that intensify awareness of gender equality and female self-determination.

Certainly for African-Americans the institutionalization of Black Studies provided a space where the hegemony of imperialist white-supremacist thought could be challenged. In the late sixties and early seventies, students, myself included, were radicalized in classrooms by coming to critical consciousness about the way dominator thinking had shaped what we knew. As a girl I had initially believed white teachers who told me we did not read black authors because they had not written any books or any good books. As a critically thinking college student I learned to interrogate the source of information. In 1969 June Jordan published the essay "Black Studies: Bringing Back the Person." She argued that Black Studies was a counter-hegemonic location for decolonized black people, writing: ". . . Black students, looking for the truth, demand teachers least likely to lie, least likely to perpetuate the traditions of lying; lies that deface the father from the memory of the child. We request Black teachers of Black studies. It is not that we believe only Black people can understand the black experience . . . For us there is nothing optional about 'Black Experience' and/or 'Black Studies:' we must know ourselves . . . We look for community. We have already suffered the alternative to community, to human commitment. We have borne the whiplash of 'white studies' . . . therefore, we cannot, in sanity, pass by the potentiality of 'Black Studies'—studies of the person consecrated to the preservation of that person." This was a powerful message about the decolonization of ways of knowing, liberating knowledge from the chokehold of white-supremacist interpretation and thought. In this essay Jordan raised the vital question: "Is the university prepared to teach us something new?" From the onset the presence of Black Studies created a context for a counter-narrative, one in which learning could take place that did not reinforce white supremacy.

In the wake of the success of militant black anti-racist work, feminist movement emerged. Since well-educated white women with class privilege were uniquely situated to enter the academy via affirmative action policies in far greater numbers than black people, they were in turn able to make affirmative action boost their numbers. As the most immediate beneficiaries of affirmative action, their inclusion served to enhance "white power and privilege" whether they were anti-racist or not. When jobs in the academy, created via the civil rights-inspired affirmative action policies went to white female candidates, white males in power could present themselves as addressing discrimination without really making way for ethnic diversity, or for the inclusion of larger groups of people of color. Feminist women, largely white, who came into the academic workforce in large numbers from the late sixties and on into the eighties, who were radicalized by feminist consciousness raising, challenged patriarchy and really begin to demand changes in curriculum so that it would no longer reflect gender biases. White male academics were far more willing to address gender equality than they were racial equality. *From bell's perspective*

Feminist intervention was amazingly successful when it came to changing academic curriculum. For example, it was not Black Studies which led to the recovery of previously unrecognized black women writers like Zora Neale Hurston. Feminist scholars, and this includes black women, were the ones who resurrected "herstory," calling attention to patriarchal exclusion of women and thus creating the awareness that led to greater inclusion. Even though I began my teaching in Black Studies, the courses I taught that were always packed with students (I had to turn students away) were those focused on women writers. The feminist challenge to patriarchal curriculum and patriarchal teaching practices completely altered the classroom. Since colleges and universities rely on students "buying" the commodity "courses" to survive, as more students flocked to courses where teaching practices as well as curriculum were not biased, where education as the practice of freedom was more the norm, the authority of the traditional white male power structure was being successfully undermined. By joining the campaign to change the curriculum, white males were able to maintain their positions of power. For example, if a racist patriarchal English professor teaching a course on William Faulkner that was a required course with many students attending, had to compete with a similar course being taught by a feminist anti-racist professor, his class could end up with no students. Hence it was in the interest of his survival for him to revise his perspective, at least to include a discussion of gender or a feminist analysis.

As an insurrection of subjugated knowledges, feminist interventions within the academic world had greater impact than Black Studies because white women could appeal to the larger, white female student population. From the onset Black Studies mainly addressed a student constituency made up of black students; feminist studies from the onset addressed white students. Even though Women's Studies courses initially attracted mostly white female students, usually those with some degree of radical consciousness, as gender equality became more an accepted norm the feminist classroom has grown larger and has attracted a diverse body of white students and students of color. Significantly, feminist professors, unlike most non-feminist Black Studies professors, were much more innovative and progressive in their teaching styles. Students often flocked in droves to feminist classrooms because the schooling there was simply more academically compelling. If this had not been the case it would not have become necessary for mainstream conservative white academics, female and male, to launch a backlash that maligned the Women's Studies classroom, falsely presenting it as teaching students that they did not need to study anything by white males and insisting that students really had to do no work in these classes. By devaluing the feminist classroom they made students feel that they would appear academically suspect if they majored in these alternative disciplines. Of course, the feminist classroom was a rigorous place of learning, and as a bonus the teaching style in such classrooms was often less conventional.

No matter the intensity of anti-feminist backlash or conservative efforts to dismantle Black Studies and Women's Studies programs, the interventions had taken place and had created enormous changes. As individual black women/women of color, along with individual white women allies in anti-racist struggle, brought a critique of race and racism into feminist thinking that transformed feminist scholarship, many of the concerns of Black Studies were addressed through a partnership with Women's Studies and through feminist scholarship. Over time, as the academy shifted, making the reforms needed to embrace inclusion—gender equality and diversity—feminist and/or black scholars were not necessarily situated only in alternative programs. The mainstreaming of progressive feminist professors and/or black professors/professors of color—that is, taking them out of the "ghetto" of Women's Studies or Ethnic Studies (which happened because white men wanted to regain their control over these disciplines)—gave them back control, but it also meant that it brought dissident voices into the conventional disciplines. Those voices changed the nature of academic discourse.

Very little praise is given Women's Studies, Black Studies/Ethnic Studies, for the amazing changes these disciplines spearheaded in higher education. When progressive white men created the alternative discipline of cultural studies, teaching from progressive standpoints, the success of their programs tended to overshadow the powerful interventions made by women and men of color simply because of the way white-supremacist thinking and practice rewards white male interventions while making it appear that the progressive interventions made by women and men of color are not as important. Since cultural studies often included recognition of race and gender, even as it allowed for the maintenance of the hegemony of white male presence, it unwittingly became one of the forces that led colleges and universities to dismantle Ethnic Studies and Women's Studies programs with the argument that they were simply no longer needed. The overall mainstreaming of alternative disciplines and alternative perspectives was a tactic deployed to take away the concrete locations of power where different policy and educational strategy could be enacted because folks did not have to rely on the conservative mainstream for promotion and tenure. Well, all that has changed. Successful backlash undermining progressive changes has changed things back to the way they were. White male rule is intact. All over our nation, Women's Studies and Ethnic Studies' programs have been ruthlessly dismantled.

Conservative manipulation of mass media has successfully encouraged parents and students to fear alternative ways of thinking, to believe that simply taking a Women's Studies course or an Ethnic Studies course will lead to failure, to not getting a job. These tactics have harmed the movement for progressive education as the practice of freedom, but they have not changed the reality that incredible progress was made. In *Teaching Values* Ron Scapp reminds us: "The antagonism toward and fear of those who 'question' had a long (and violent) history. That those asking questions today and rejecting the 'givens' of our cultural history are seen as pariahs and are under attack should also not be 'surprising.' " Scapp calls attention to the fact that the folks who resist progressive educational reform "are quick to dismiss or discredit (and sometimes destroy)," but this does not alter the fact that there has been a powerful meaningful insurrection of subjugated knowledges that is liberating and life-sustaining.

Struggles for gender equality and ethnic diversity linked issues of ending domination, of social justice with pedagogy. The classroom was transformed. The critique of canons allowed the voices of visionary intellectuals to be heard. Gayatri Spivak brilliantly challenged the notions that only citizens of this nation can know and understand the importance of the traditional canon. Daringly she states: "The matter of the literary canon is in fact a political matter: securing authority." In *Outside in the Teaching Machine* she explains the importance of "transnational literacy," starting with a discussion of the high school classroom. Writing about the canon, Spivak contends that she "must speak from within the debate over the teaching of canon," from a perspective informed by postcolonial awareness of the need to create justice in education: "There can be no general theory of canons. Canons are the condition of institutions and the effect of institutions. Canons secure institutions as institutions secure canons . . . Since it is indubitably the case that there is no expansion without contraction . . . [W]e must make room for the coordinated teaching of the new entries into the canon. When I bring this up, I hear stories of how undergraduates have told their teachers that a whole semester of Shakespeare, or Milton, or Chaucer, changed their lives. I do not doubt these stories, but we have to do a quality/quantity shift if we are going to canonize the new entries . . . The undergraduates will have their lives changed perhaps by a sense of the diversity of the new canon and the unacknowledged power play involved in securing the old." Spivak's work, emerging from a transnational, feminist, anti-racist, left critique, embodies the extraordinary genius and power of the intellectual interventions transforming the old academy.

Obviously, despite interventions, much about the academy did not change. However, that does not render the changes any less relevant or awesome. Whereas the conventional dominator classroom remained a place where students were simply given material to learn by rote and regurgitate, students in the progressive classroom were learning how to think critically. They were learning to open their minds. And the more they expanded their critical consciousness the less likely they were to support ideologies of domination. Progressive professors did not need to indoctrinate students and teach them that they should oppose domination. Students came to these positions via their own capacity to think critically and assess the world they live in. Progressive educators discussing issues of imperialism, race, gender, class, and sexuality heightened everyone's awareness of the importance of these concerns (even those individuals who did not agree with our perspective). That awareness has created the conditions for concrete change, even if those conditions are not yet known to everyone. Certainly, in the last twenty years progressive educators, teachers, and students have positively worked on behalf of social justice, realizing the goals of democracy in ways that are awesome. Hence the backlash has been equally awesome.

Significantly the assault on progressive educators, and on new ways of knowing, was most viciously launched not by educators but by policy makers and their conservative cohorts who control mass media. The competing pedagogy, the voice of dominator hegemony, was heard around the world via the lessons taught by imperialist white-supremacist capitalist patriarchal mass media. While the academic world became a place where humanitarian dreams could be realized through education as the practice of freedom via a pedagogy of hope, the world outside was busily teaching people the need to maintain injustice, teaching fear and violence, teaching terrorism. The critique of "otherness" spearheaded by progressive educators was not as powerful as conservative mass media's insistence that otherness must be acknowledged, hunted down, destroyed. In *Hatreds: Racialized and Sexualized Conflicts in the Twenty-First Century*, Zillah Eisenstein explains in the chapter "Writing Hatred on the Body": "On the eve of the twenty-first century, hatreds explode in such places as Sarajevo, Argentina, Chechnya, Rwanda, Los Angeles, and Oklahoma City. The hatred embodies a complex set of fears about difference and otherness. It reveals what some people fear in themselves, their own 'differences.' Hatred forms around the unknown, the difference of 'others.' And we have learned the difference that we fear through racialized and sexualized markings. Because people grow othered by their racialized sexualized and engendered bodies, bodies are important to the writing of hatred on history." Academic challenges to this hatred, though meaningful, do not reach enough of our nation's citizens.

When the tragic events of 9/11 occurred it was as though, in just a few moments in time, all our work to end domination in all its forms, all our pedagogies of hope, were rendered meaningless as much of the American public, reacting to the news coverage of the tragedy, responded with an outpouring of imperialist white-supremacist nationalist capitalist patriarchal rage against terrorists defined as dark-skinned others even when there were no images, no concrete proof. That rage spilled over into everyday hatred of people of color from all races in this nation, as Muslims from all walks of life found themselves rebuked and scorned—the objects of a random and reckless violence. No matter the overwhelming majority of people of color whose lives were tragically lost on 9/11, the more than sixty countries represented, every religion in the world represented, innocents of all shapes, sizes, colors, the newborn and the old— cruel Western cultural imperialism reduced this brutal massacre to the simply binary of "us/them," of United States citizens as "the chosen people" against a world full of "unchosen" people. Thankfully, among colleagues and comrades who know better, individual people of color hoped first to grieve, then to talk of justice. Whenever we love justice and stand on the side of justice we refuse simplistic binaries. We refuse to allow either/or thinking to cloud our judgment. We embrace the logic of both/and. We acknowledge the limits of what we know.

Even though I could walk to the sites of the 9/11 tragedy, I was not able to speak about these events for some time because I had come face-to-face with the limits of what I know. I could not be a critic of imperialist white-supremacist capitalist patriarchal mass media, then rely on it to teach me about what had taken place. What I knew, the limits of my knowing, was defined by information in alternative mass media and by the boundaries of what I experienced, of all that I witnessed. That's all I could account for. Anything more would have been interpretations of interpretations offered me by a media whose agenda I hold suspect.

From the moment of the attacks and then in the days and weeks afterwards, our neighborhoods were fenced off. Only the sounds of planes could be heard. Only the state enforcers, the police walked freely. Men, mainly white men, with guns were everywhere. Everywhere people of color were randomly targeted. As soon as they could, the privileged folks in our neighborhoods (mostly white) left for their country homes. Neighbors called me from their houses hours away to give me the news. Friends and comrades from all over the world called to grieve and to lament. I felt surrounded by caring communities. Yet racial hatred, coming from folks who had always presented themselves as critically conscious, was as intense as that coming from groups who have had no concern for justice, who are not even able to acknowledge that our nation is an imperialist white-supremacist capitalist patriarchy. It was a moment of utter chaos where the seeds of fascist ideology were bearing fruit everywhere. In our nations, schools, and colleges, free speech

lost promotions
really?

?

gave way to censorship. Individuals lost their jobs or lost promotions because they dared to express the right to dissent that is a
core civil right in a democratic society. All over our nation, citizens were stating that they were willing to give up civil rights to
ensure that this nation would win the war against terrorism.

In a matter of months many citizens ceased to believe in the
value of living in diverse communities, of anti-racist work, of seeking peace. They surrendered their belief in the healing power of
justice. Hardcore white-supremacist nationalism reared its ugly
voice and spoke openly, anywhere. Individuals who dared to dissent, to critique, to challenge misinformation were and are
labeled traitors. As time passed, we witnessed a mounting backlash against any individual or group who dared to work for justice, who opposed domination in all its forms.

A profound cynicism is at the core of dominator culture
wherever it prevails in the world. At this time in our lives, citizens all around the world feel touched by death-dealing cynicism that normalizes violence, that makes war and tells us that
peace is not possible, that it can especially not be realized
among those who are different, who do not look or sound
alike, who do not eat the same food, worship the same gods, or
speak the same language. Since much of the pedagogy of domination is brought to us in the United States by mass media,
particularly via television, I rarely watch TV. No one, no matter
how intelligent and skillful at critical thinking, is protected
against the subliminal suggestions that imprint themselves on
our unconscious brain if we are watching hours and hours of
television. In the United States television has become primarily
a series of spectacles that perpetuate and maintain the ideology of imperialist white-supremacist capitalist patriarchy.
There have been times in the history of the United States when
the media have been a location where diverse voices are heard
despite the hegemony of more conservative forces.

Right now, free speech and the right to dissent are being
undermined by conservative, mass media-pushing dominator

culture. The message of dominator culture would have little impact if it were not for the power of mass media to seductively magnify that message. For example, much of the television coverage of 9/11 focused on firefighters who are predominantly white males. New York firefighters have had notoriously racist hiring practices. Many Americans saw the victims of the 9/11 tragedy as white. Had the focus been on the victims of the tragedy, not just the portraits of privileged rich, white individuals who lost their lives, whose deaths are still tragic, but on the masses of poor working people who were slaughtered, a huge majority of them non-American people of color, the conservative "us/them" agendas would not have so easily become the popular response. If mass media had chosen to focus on the incredible national and religious diversity of the victims of 9/11 (including the many Muslims who were killed), it would have been impossible to create the sentimental narrative of us against them, of Americans against the world. In fact, the world's diversity was embodied in the people killed on 9/11. It was never a uniquely American tragedy, but television distorted truths to make it appear that this was so. And lots of viewers who would ordinarily know better were seduced because of the way in which grief created a context of vulnerability and rage where folks were eager to simplify everything to make a common enemy.

Our senses are assaulted by the stench of domination every day, here in the places where we live. No wonder, then, that so many people feel terribly confused, uncertain, and without hope. More than anywhere else a dominator-controlled mass media, with its constant manipulation of representations in the service of the status quo, assaults us in that place where we would know hope. Despair is the greatest threat. When despair prevails we cannot create life-sustaining communities of resistance. Paulo Friere reminds us that "without a vision for tomorrow hope is impossible." Our visions for tomorrow are most vital when they emerge from the concrete circumstances of change we are experiencing right now.

Teach 2

Time Out

Classrooms without Boundaries

Although for most of my teaching career the university class-room has been an exhilarating place, in recent years I have begun to feel a need for significant time away from my job. I was burning out. Entering the classroom at the big city university where I taught, I began to feel as though I was entering a prison, a closed-down space where, no matter how hard I tried, it was difficult to create a positive context for learning. At first I blamed my sense of gloom on the size of the classroom, the gap in skill and aptitude of my students, the intensified spying on the part of administration and faculty (usually taking the form of grilling students about what happened in my class-rooms, and on the basis of their comments, giving me unwanted critical feedback). In actuality, these obstacles had always been a part of my teaching experience. My capacity to cope with them in a constructive ways was diminishing. I needed time away from teaching.

All teachers—in every teaching situation from kindergarten to university settings—need time away from teaching at some point in their career. The amount of time is relative. Certainly, the many unemployed teachers, especially at the college level, could all work some of the time if teachers everywhere, in every educational system, were allowed to take unpaid leaves whenever they desired. At the city university where I was a tenured distinguished professor when my contract was first negotiated, it was agreed that I could take unpaid leaves to do writing and research. The salary I was paid could have covered the hiring of two or three faculty members new to teaching. Even though I negotiated this agreement, when I wanted to take a leave it was difficult to attain permission from deans, faculty, and administration. Some folks were worried that agreeing to unpaid leaves when requested would mean that all the stellar faculty would be constantly away. This seemed like a bogus argument. If we all had had incomes that allowed us to be away constantly, we would never have needed teaching jobs in the first place. Even if all college teachers had the opportunity to take unpaid leave whenever they desired, the vast majority do not have the economic means to negatively exploit this opportunity. Consulting with teachers on every educational level, I find that most of us want time out when we desperately need it, when we are just feeling burnt out and are unable to make the classroom a constructive setting for learning.

The classroom is one of the most dynamic work settings precisely because we are given such a short amount of time to do so much. To perform with excellence and grace teachers must be totally present in the moment, totally concentrated and focused. When we are not fully present, when our minds are elsewhere, our teaching is diminished. I knew it was time for me to take a break from the classroom when my mind was always someplace else. And in the last stages of burnout, I knew I needed to be someplace else because I just simply did not want to get up, get dressed, and go to work. I dreaded the classroom. The most negative consequence of this type of burnout is manifest when teachers begin to abhor and hate students. This happens. When I met recently with grade-school teachers, one woman boldly testified that she felt the classroom situation had become insane, that size and disciplinary issues were just making it impossible for her to teach. She hated her job and her students.

I suggested that she take time to examine her circumstances and identify any aspect of the teaching experience that she still finds compelling joyful. Yet she crudely and cynically let the group know that she was no longer open to finding anything positive about her job. To her it is, was, and will be the job she will continue to do to maintain the material lifestyle she finds desirable. Surprised when I suggested that maybe it was time for her to imagine, and then look for, work that she would find more meaningful, she let the group know she has accepted that there is no way out. She feels doomed, condemned to stay in the prison of work she no longer wants to do. And of course the students she teaches are also condemned, compelled to remain in a setting where the only hope of learning is the gaining of information from formulaic lesson plans.

This person's cynicism about teaching is a commonly held attitude. She was daring enough to give voice to sentiments that many teachers feel. And sadly, it is often the public school setting where the sense of hopelessness about teaching is the most intense and widespread. Understanding that there are times when we "must work for money rather than meaning," educator Parker Palmer describes in *The Courage to Teach* the way continuing to work at any vocation, but particularly teaching, when we are no longer positively engaged does violence to the self "in the precise sense that it violates my integrity and identity . . . When I violate myself, I invariably end up violating the people I work with. How many teachers inflict their own pain on their students, the pain that comes from doing what never was, or no longer is, their true work."

Public school teachers feel extremely confined by classroom size and set lesson plans where they have little choice about the content of the material they are required to teach. And if required standardized testing is institutionalized anew, it will be even harder for public school teachers to bring creative ideas to the work of teaching. They will be required simply to relay information as though the work they do is akin to that of any worker on an assembly line.

When I left my teaching job to take two years off with unpaid leave, I did not leave teaching settings. In order to survive economically, I worked the lecture circuit. It was a refreshing change, because usually the folks who attended my lectures came because they were open to hearing what I had to say and open to learning. This was different from teaching in a classroom setting where a substantial number of students inform you on the first day of class that they are there not because they are interested in the subject but because they needed to take all their classes on a Tuesday and your class time was a perfect fit. And of course the big difference in giving lectures is the absence of grading. Like many teachers I found grading to be one of the most stressful aspects of teaching. Grading has become even more stressful in a world where students determine that they need to make a specific grade to be successful and want to be awarded that grade irrespective of their performance.

Understanding grading to be an evaluation of a student's learning capacity and output, I worked through my tensions around grading by teaching students to apply the criteria that would be used to grade them and then to grade themselves so that they could remain aware of their ability to do needed work at the level of achievement they desired. At different intervals, in one-on-one settings, their self-evaluations would be placed alongside my evaluation. The difficult part of this process was teaching students to be rigorous and critical in their self-evaluations. But more often than not our grading would be the same.

Just as I evaluated my students in each class I taught, I evaluated myself. Continual self-evaluation was the experience that made my burnout more apparent and intense. Just as students whose grade shifts from an A to a C feel bad, I felt bad when I felt that my teaching was not consistently A+. When I first began to feel the need for a time-out I shared my concerns with beloved students who persuaded me for a time that my teaching on a "bad" day was still far more productive than most of their classes. They knew that many of the job-related issues causing me stress were not classroom related. Working within an educational system wherein the faculty was 90 percent white and the student body 90 percent non-white, a system wherein both the banking system of education and racially biased notions of brilliance and genius prevailed, I felt alienated from colleagues. Many of my colleagues were well-meaning liberals who worked overtime at their teaching tasks and who were simply unenlightened when it came to issue of race. Although well-meaning, they unknowingly often perpetuated racist stereotypes, claiming that the presence of so many non-white students, a great many of them foreigners, had lowered standards. Concurrently, they believed they had to lower their standards to teach these "backward students."

I came to teach at a big city university located in a diverse non-white community after years of teaching at predominantly white elite schools. Since I had always planned to retire from teaching early I wanted to spend what I believed would be my last years of teaching at a school that would enable me to teach students coming from poor and working-class backgrounds similar to my own. My first full time assistant professor teaching position was at Yale University. It was a wonderful teaching experience because the students who came to my classrooms, who chose to were unique and different. They were deeply committed to learning, to excelling academically, to doing rigorous work. They were a joy to teach.

When I chose to teach at a big state school, many of my colleagues warned me that I would be disappointed by the students, that I would find myself "teaching down." These warnings came from colleagues who taught at elite schools, and they were echoed by my new colleagues. I found that my students at this public institution were just as brilliant and open to learning as my beloved Yalies, but that the difference was often in levels of self-esteem. Low self-esteem led many a brilliant student in Harlem to self-sabotage. It was difficult for me to "lose" students who were excellent. For example: A really hardworking gifted student doing excellent work might simply stop attending class in the last few weeks. When I taught at elite private schools, where most students lived on campus or nearby, if I faced such a problem it was easy to locate a student (even if it meant knocking on their door at home) to seek an explanation and a solution to problems. This process could not happen at a commuter school where students often lived two or three hours away. Locating a student often took hours of time. And by the time a connection was made it was too late for grades reflecting excellence.

I taught predominantly non-white students from poor and working-class backgrounds, most of them parents, and many of them doing the work of full-time single parenting, working a job, and attending school. This required of me constant vigilance when it came to maintaining standards of excellence in the classroom. From my own position of class privilege (being single and childless) the opportunity to feel sorry for students whose circumstances were difficult was constant. It was often hard to face their pain and hardship and remind them that they had made the choice to be a student and were therefore accountable to the demands and responsibilities required of them. Their task, I told them, was to learn how to do excellent work while coping with myriad responsibilities. And if they could not excel then their task was to give their very best and make peace with the outcome. I too had to make peace with the outcome. Just as it was often emotionally difficult for students, it was emotionally difficult for their beloved teacher.

I use the word beloved here, not to be immodest, but to describe the truth of my experience. I felt beloved by most of my students. They were grateful to me for believing in them, for educating them for the practice of freedom, for urging them to become critical thinkers able to make responsible choices. Their appreciation of my teaching was a force that kept me wedded to the classroom long past the moment when I felt I needed to separate, to leave. Teaching with excellence and being rewarded for this work by excellent student work is a truly ecstatic experience. Leaving the classroom, I was leaving behind the emotional and academic intensity of that experience. Parker Palmer's words resonated for me: "As good teachers weave the fabric that joins them with students and subjects, the heart is the loom on which the threads are tried, the tension is held, the shuttle flies, and the fabric is stretched tight. Small wonder, then, that teaching tugs at the heart, opens the heart, even breaks the heart—and the more one loves teaching, the more heartbreaking it can be. The courage to teach is the courage to keep one's heart open in those very moments when the heart is asked to hold more than it is able so that teacher and students and subject can be woven into the fabric of community that learning, and living, require." It takes courage for any teacher who teaches with gladness to accept and respond to periods of burnout, to embrace the heartache of loss and separation.

To use another of my sports metaphors, I often felt like that player who threatens retirement but never leaves. Or who leaves but comes back. Observing myself become dispirited and tired of teaching, I knew that it was time for me to take a break or even leave the classroom forever. And yet it was difficult to come to terms with being a great teacher, loving students, yet feeling a desperate need to leave the world of academe in all its ramifications. Working within the conventional corporate academic world where the primary goals of institutions is to sell education and produce a professional managerial class schooled in the art of obedience to authority and accepting of dominator-based hierarchy, I often felt as though I was in the dysfunctional family of my childhood where I was often in the outsider position and scapegoated, viewed as both mad and yet a threat. To regain my sense of full integrity as a self, I needed to leave the academy, to remove from my life the constant pressure to conform or to endure punishment for non-conformity.

I used my leave time to see if I could survive despite the huge drop in income that would take place if I left my job. During the first six months of absenting myself from academe, from the classroom, I felt a profound sense of loss. For more than twenty years the rhythms of my life had been set by the cycles of semesters ending and beginning, by school holidays, and summers off. Suddenly I was in a world where every day was a day off. And it did not feel empowering. I had to face being without the magic of the classroom and the caring community of learners I had dwelled in for most of my adult life, being always either student or teacher. Like many retirees I suddenly felt as though I was cut off from a system that had been a form of life support. Without it, life felt less interesting, less compelling. I was the teacher alone with myself, the teacher facing myself as the pupil, needing to chart a new journey for myself. Teaching filled huge spaces in my life, and my engagement with students was a space of emotional intensity and intimacy that was fundamentally altered by my leaving the classroom.

Initially, I spent my months away from the classroom contemplating where I needed to be. I lingered in that contemplative space which Palmer defines as "an inner emptiness in which new truth, often alien and unsettling truth, can emerge." In *The Active Life* Palmer writes about the empowerment that can emerge when we shift a set position, when we dislocate, explaining: "If disillusionment is one of life's natural forms of contemplation, the experience of dislocation is another. This happens when we are forced by circumstance to occupy a very different standpoint from our normal one, and our angle of vision suddenly changes to reveal a strange and threatening landscape. . . . The value of dislocation, like the value of disillusionment, is in the way that it moves us beyond illusion, so we can see reality in the round—since what we are able to see depends entirely on where we stand." Away from the corporate university classroom, from teaching in a degree-centered context, I was able to focus more on the practice of teaching and learning. I especially began to contemplate those forms of teaching and learning that take place outside the structured classroom.

Despite my criticism of the banking system of education, I had unwittingly been seduced by the notion of the set classroom time as the most useful vehicle to teach and learn. Dislocated, with time on my hands to contemplate being outside the structured classroom, I began to think of new ways to be immersed in teaching. Dislocation is the perfect context for free-flowing thought that lets us move beyond the restricted confines of a familiar social order.

Like many individuals seeking a new path, I pondered what I would do in the world of teaching and learning if I were free to design and choose. My first awareness was that I did not want to teach in settings where students were not fully committed to our shared learning experience. I did not want to teach in settings where individuals needed to be graded. To me the best context for teaching was, of course, one where students chose to come because they wanted to learn, from me, from one another. Rather than teaching for semesters I wanted to be immersed in short intense learning workshops where attention is concentrated and focused. I wanted to teach about teaching, about the ways classrooms settings can be a place where we all learn the practice of freedom. Teaching and learning in the direction of justice, peace, and love, of creating and maintaining academic and or intellectual community, became the vocational goals I wanted to pursue. And as I began to speak these longings, individuals responded with job requests.

When my two-year leave ended, I resigned. Reluctantly, I let go of the safety net of tenure and organized interactions with educational colleagues. Leaving my academic job raised the fear that as an intellectual in an anti-intellectual society I would be all the more isolated.

Being an intellectual is not the same as being an academic. There is tremendous support in our society for the academic life for those who are insiders inside. Indeed, as those of us who have been privy to countless discussions about the differences between the academy and the so called "real" world know, many professors see themselves as members of a chosen group, a large secret society, elitist and hierarchical, that sets them apart. Even though colleges and universities have a corporate infrastructure, that power is usually masked. Most faculty choose denial over conscious awareness of the way crude economic policies shape academic environments.

As an intellectual working as an academic I often felt that my commitment to radical openness and devotion to critical thinking, to seeking after truth, was at odds with the demands that I uphold the status quo if I wanted to be rewarded. My integrity was as much at risk in the academic world as it had been in the non-academic work world, where workers are expected to obey authority and follow set rules. While much lip service is given to the notion of free speech in academic settings, in actuality constant censorship—often self-imposed—takes place. Teachers fear they will not receive promotions or that in worst-case scenarios they will lose their jobs. Even so, in our society the academic world remains the primary place where teaching and learning are valued, where reading and thinking are deemed meaningful and necessary work. This validation, however limited in scope, provides affirmation and sustenance for academics and/or intellectuals in an anti-intellectual culture.

Cutting my secure ties to academic institutions, I faced the challenge of finding and creating spaces where teaching and learning could be practiced outside the norm. Like many professors I naively believed that the more I moved up the academic ladder the more freedom I would gain, only to find that greater academic success carried with it even more pressure to conform, to ally oneself with institutional goals and values rather than with intellectual work. I felt enormously lucky that I was able to succeed in the academic world as a radical, dissident thinker. My success, like that of other lucky individuals whose thinking goes against the norm, was a constant reminder of the reality that there are no closed systems, that every system has a gap and that in that space is a place of possibility. All over our nation, conservative repressive institutions are vocational homes for those rare individuals who do not conform, who are committed to education as the practice of freedom.

Seeking places outside formal educational settings to teach and learn, I found it possible to make critical interventions in a number of ways. I began doing visits to public schools, mostly pushed into service in this manner by family and friends. My sister G., a grade school teacher in the Flint, Michigan school system, has always urged me to come and talk with her students. Like many folks accustomed solely to teaching in university settings, I was comfortable talking with and teaching adults, but I was afraid I lacked the skills to engage in meaningful dialogue with children. Persuading me that this was nonsense, that I could do it, G. let me loose in her classrooms and in auditoriums filled with third- and fourth-graders. This work was challenging. It was not paid labor. This experience, and the many more that followed it let me know that if one is willing to work without pay there are many formal educational settings that will welcome informal teaching interventions.

In the last few years I have been doing work for pay within a number of formal educational settings. Teaching intensive courses for a week or a month to professors and students enabled, and enables, me to engage in education as the practice of freedom without restrictions or fear of punishing reprisals. This is an utterly rewarding experience. I understand fully Palmer's assertion: "I am a teacher at heart, and there are moments in the classroom when I can hardly hold the joy." My leaving a high-ranking tenured position opened up new spaces for teaching and learning that renewed and restored my spirit and enabled me to hold onto the joy in teaching that makes my heart glad.

Teach 3

Talking Race and Racism

Teachers are often among that group most reluctant to acknowledge the extent to which white-supremacist thinking informs every aspect of our culture including the way we learn, the content of what we learn, and the manner in which we are taught. Much of the consciousness-raising around the issue of white supremacy and racism has focused attention on teaching what racism is and how it manifests itself in the daily workings of our lives. In anti-racist workshops and seminars, much of the time is often spent simply breaking through the denial that leads many unenlightened white people, as well as people of color, to pretend that racist and white-supremacist thought and action are no longer pervasive in our culture.

In classroom settings I have often listened to groups of students tell me that racism really no longer shapes the contours of our lives, that there is just no such thing as racial difference, that "we are all just people." Then a few minutes later I give them an exercise. I ask if they were about to die and could choose to come back as a white male, a white female, a black female, or black male, which identity would they choose. Each time I do this exercise, most individuals, irrespective of gender or race invariably choose whiteness, and most often white maleness. Black females are the least chosen. When I ask students to explain their choice they proceed to do a sophisticated analysis of privilege based on race (with perspectives that take gender and class into consideration). This disconnect between their conscious repudiation of race as a marker of privilege and their unconscious understanding is a gap we have to bridge, an illusion that must be shattered before a meaningful discussion of race and racism can take place. This exercise helps them to move past their denial of the existence of racism. It lets us begin to work together toward a more unbiased approach to knowledge.

Teaching, lecturing, and facilitating workshops and writing about ending racism and other forms of domination, I have found that confronting racial biases, and more important, white-supremacist thinking, usually requires that all of us take a critical look at what we learned early in life about the nature of race. Those initial imprints seem to overdetermine attitudes about race. In writing groups we often begin simply with our first remembered awareness of race. Exploring our earliest ways of knowing about race, we find it easier to think about the question of standpoint. Individual white people, moving from denial of race to awareness, suddenly realize that white-supremacist culture encourages white folks to deny their understanding of race, to claim as part of their superiority that they are *beyond* thinking about race. Yet when the denial stops, it becomes clear that underneath their skin most white folks have an intimate awareness of the politics of race and racism. They have learned to pretend that it is not so, to take on the posture of learned helplessness.

It has become more fashionable, and at times profitable, for white folks in academic environments to think and write about race. It is as though the very act of thinking about the nature of race and racism is still seen as "dirty" work best suited for black folks and other people of color or a form of privileged "acting out" for anti-racist white folks. Black folks/people of color who talk too much about race are often represented by the racist mindset as "playing the race card" (note how this very expression trivializes discussions of racism, implying it's all just a game), or as simply insane. White folks who talk race, however, are often represented as patrons, as superior civilized beings. Yet their actions are just another indication of white-supremacist power, as in "we are so much more civilized and intelligent than black folks/people of color that we know better than they do all that can be understood about race."

Simply talking about race, white supremacy, and racism can lead one to be typecast, excluded, placed lower on the food chain in the existing white-supremacist system. No wonder then that such talk can become an exercise in powerlessness because of the way it is filtered and mediated by those who hold the power to both control public speech (via editing, censorship, modes of representation, and interpretation). While more individuals in contemporary culture talk about race and racism, the power of that talk has been diminished by racist backlash that trivializes it, more often than not representing it as mere hysteria.

Individual black people/people of color often describe moments where they challenge racist speech at meetings or in other formal settings only to witness a majority of folks rush to comfort the racist individual they have challenged, as though that person is the victim and the person who raised questions a persecutor. No wonder then that while discussions of white supremacy and racism have become rather commonplace in individual scholarly writing and journalistic work, most people are wary, if not downright fearful, of discussing these issues in group settings, especially when among strangers. People often tell me that they do not share openly and candidly their thoughts about white-supremacist thought and racism for fear that they will say the wrong thing. And yet when this reason is interrogated it usually is shown to cover up the fear of conflict, the belief that saying the wrong thing will generate conflict, bad feeling, or lead to counterattack. Groups where white folks are in the majority often insist that race and racism does not really have much meaning in today's world because we are all so beyond caring about it. I ask them why they then have so much fear about speaking their minds. Their fear, their censoring silence, is indicative of the loaded meaning race and racism have in our society.

One of the bitter ironies anti-racists face when working to end white-supremacist thinking and action is that the folks who most perpetuate it are the individuals who are usually the least willing to acknowledge that race matters. In almost all the writing I have done on the topics of race, I state my preference for using the word white supremacy to describe the system of race-based biases we live within because this term, more than racism, is inclusive of everyone. It encompasses black people/people of color who have a racist mindset, even though they may organize their thinking and act differently from racist whites. For example: a black female who has internalized racism may straighten her hair to appear more like white females. And yet this same individual might become irate if any white person were to praise her for wanting to be white. She might confront them about being racist while remaining in complete denial about her allegiance to white-supremacist thinking about the nature of beauty. It may be just as difficult to break through this person's denial about her collusion with white-supremacist thinking as to try to create awareness in a racist white person. Most people in our nation oppose overt acts of racist terror or violence. We are a nation of citizens who claim that they want to see an end to racism, to racial discrimination. Yet there is clearly a fundamental gap between theory and practice. No wonder, then, that it has been easier for everyone in our nation to accept a critical written discourse about racism that is usually read only by those who have some degree of educational privilege than it is for us to create constructive ways to talk about white supremacy and racism, to find constructive actions that go beyond talk.

In more recent years, as discourses about race and racism have been accepted in academic settings, individual black people/people of color have been to some extent psychologically terrorized by the bizarre gaps between theory and practice. For example: a well-meaning liberal white female professor might write a useful book on the intersections of race and gender yet continue to allow racist biases to shape the manner in which she responds personally to women of color. . . . She may have a "grandiose" sense of herself, that is, a confidence that she is anti-racist and not all vigilant about making the connections that would transform her behavior and not just her thinking. When it comes to the subject of race and racism, many folks once naively believed that if we could change the way people thought we would change their behavior. Move often than not, *More* this has not been the case. Yet we should not be profoundly dismayed by this. In a culture of domination almost everyone engages in behaviors that contradict their beliefs and values. This is why some sociologists and psychologists are writing about the reality that in our nation individuals lie more and more about all manner of things large and small. This lying often leads to forms of denial wherein individuals are unable to distinguish between fantasy and fact, between wishful dreaming and reality.

While it is a positive aspect of our culture that folks want to see racism end; paradoxically it is this heartfelt longing that underlies the persistence of the false assumption that racism has ended, that this in not a white-supremacist nation. In our culture almost everyone, irrespective of skin color, associates white supremacy with extreme conservative fanaticism, with Nazi skinheads who preach all the old stereotypes about racist purity. Yet these extreme groups rarely threaten the day-to-day workings of our lives. It is the less extreme white supremacists' beliefs and assumptions, easier to cover up and mask, that maintain and perpetuate everyday racism as a form of group oppression.

Once we can face all the myriad ways white-supremacist thinking shapes our daily perceptions, we can understand the reasons liberal whites who are concerned with ending racism may simultaneously hold on to beliefs and assumptions that have their roots in white supremacy. We can also face the way black people/people of color knowingly and unknowingly internalize white-supremacist thinking. In a class I was teaching recently, we discussed a talk I had given where many white students expressed their disdain for the ideas I expressed, and for my presence, by booing. I challenged the group to consider that what I was saying was not as disturbing to the group as was my embodied young-looking presence, a black female with natural hair in braids. I had barely finished this comment before a liberal white male in the group attacked claiming "you are playing the race card here." His immediate defensive response is often the feedback that comes when black people/people of color make an observation about the everyday dynamics of race and racism, sex and sexism that does not conform to privileged white perceptions.

Understanding the degree to which class privilege mediates and shapes perceptions about race is vital to any public discourse on the subject because the most privileged people in our nation (especially those with class power) are often the most unwilling to speak honestly about racist biases. Working-class whites in our nation will often speak quite eloquently about the way racist assumptions fuel our perceptions and our actions daily, while white folks from privileged class backgrounds continue to do the dance of denial, pretending that shared class privileges mediate or transform racism. I explained to the group that one of the manifestations of daily life in an imperialist white-supremacist capitalist patriarchy is that the vast majority of white folks have little intimacy with black people and are rarely in situations where they must listen to a black person (particularly a black woman) speak to them for thirty minutes. Certainly, there were no black teachers when I was an undergraduate English major and graduate student. It would not have occurred to me to look for black female teachers in other disciplines. I accepted this absence.

I shared with the class that in my daily life as a member of the upper classes, living alone in a predominantly white neighborhood and working in predominantly white settings, I have little organic contact with black females. If I wanted to talk with or listen to black women, I have to make an effort. Yet here was an upper-class white man living in a predominantly white world, working in a predominantly white setting, telling me that white folks have no trouble listening to black females teach them, listening to black females express beliefs and values that run counter to their own. I asked the group to consider why the response to my initial ideas about the rarity of white folks having to listen to black women talk and/teach was not: "Gee. I have never thought about how race determines who we listen to, who we accept as authorities." It would have been interesting had the white male colleague who vehemently disagreed withheld his comments until he had given the matter serious thought, until he was able to present cogent reasons why he disagreed with my statement. By evaluating me (i.e., suggesting I was being false and "playing the race card") he avoided having to present the fact-based and/or experiential reasons he thought differently from me. His response personalized an observation that I do not consider personal.

Given the nature of imperialist white-supremacist capitalist patriarchy as a system shaping culture and beliefs it is simply a fact that most white folks are rarely, if ever, in situations where they must listen to black women lecture to them. Even the white folks who have black maids and housekeepers working in their homes daily do not listen to these women when they talk.

This reality was graphically depicted years ago in the 1950s' box office hit, *Imitation of Life*, when Laura, the rich white woman comes to her black housekeeper/maid Annie's funeral and is awed that Annie had friends, was a highly regarded church woman, and so on. Certainly the biographies and autobiographies of white women who were raised by black female servants abound with testimony that they did not dialogue with these women, or listen to them tell their stories, or share information they did not want to hear.

We operate in a world of class privilege that remains undemocratic and discriminatory so that most upper-class black folks in white settings are isolated and must make an effort to hear black females talk and/or lecture for thirty minutes. My honest testimony to this fact was a critical intervention that created a moment of pause in the minds of those students who were not operating with closed minds. They could ponder my comments and relate them to their lives. They could ask themselves "who do I listen to?" or "whose words do I value?" I offered Oprah Winfrey as an example of a black female who daily commands the attention of masses of white folks, and yet her role is usually that of commentator. She listens and interprets the speech of others. Rarely does she express her particular views on a subject for more than a few minutes, if at all. In many ways she is seen in the racist imagination as "housekeeper/mammy," not unlike that of Annie in *Imitation of Life* whose primary goal in life is to make sure white folks can live the best possible life. Remember that for fifteen years Annie sent the old milkman her hard-earned money every Christmas pretending that it came from the selfish, rich, white woman. This was Annie's way of teaching by example. Her motivation is to make Laura a better person and, of course, by doing so she reveals what a good person she herself is.

Annie is the black woman who knows that her place is to be subordinate and to serve; she serves with acceptance, dignity, and grace. She does not confront the white mistress with ideas and critical perspectives that white females do not want to hear. This is the model offered black females by the racist, sexist imagination. That model is represented currently in almost every Hollywood representation of black womanhood. No wonder then that so many white folks find it hard to "listen" to a black woman critic speaking ideas and opinions that threaten their belief systems. In our class discussion someone pointed out that a powerful white male had given a similar talk but he was not given negative, disdainful, verbal feedback. It was not that listeners agreed with what he said; it was that they believed he had a right to state his viewpoint.

Often individual black people and/or people of color are in settings where we are the only colored person present. In such settings unenlightened white folks often behave toward us as though we are the guests and they the hosts. They act as though our presence is less a function of our skill, aptitude, genius, and more the outcome of philanthropic charity. Thinking this way, they see our presence as functioning primarily as a testament to their largesse; it tells the world they are not racist. Yet the very notion that we are there to serve them is itself an expression of white-supremacist thinking. At the core of white-supremacist thinking in the United States and elsewhere is the assumption that it is natural for the inferior races (darker people) to serve the superior races (in societies where there is no white presence, lighter-skinned people should be served by darker-skinned people). Embedded in this notion of service is that no matter what the status of the person of color, that position must be reconfigured to the greater good of whiteness.

This was an aspect of white-supremacist thinking that made the call for racial integration and diversity acceptable to many white folks. To them, integration meant having access to people of color who would either spice up their lives (the form of service we might call the performance of exotica) or provide them with the necessary tools to continue their race-based dominance (for example: the college students from privileged white homes who go to the third world to learn Spanish or Swahili for "fun," except that it neatly fits later that this skill helps them when they are seeking employment). Time and time again in classes, white students who were preparing to study or live briefly in a non-white country talk about the people in these countries as though they existed merely to enhance white adventure. Truly, their vision was not unlike that of the message white kids received from watching the racist television show *Tarzan* ("go native and enhance your life"). The beat poet Jack Kerouac expressed his sentiments in the language of cool "the best the white world had offered was not enough ecstasy for me." Just as many unaware whites, often liberal, saw and see their interactions with people of color via affirmative action as an investment that will improve their lives, even enhance their organic superiority. Many people of color, schooled in the art of internalized white-supremacist thinking, shared this assumption.

Chinese writer Anchee Min captures the essence of this worship of whiteness beautifully in *Katherine*, a novel about a young white teacher coming to China, armed with seductive cultural imperialism. Describing to one of her pupils her perception that the Chinese are a cruel people (certainly this was a popular racist stereotype in pre-twentieth century America) she incites admiration in her Chinese pupil who confesses: "Her way of thinking touched me. It was something I had forgotten or maybe had never known. She unfolded the petals of my dry heart. A flower I did not know existed began to bloom inside me . . . Katherine stretched my life beyond its own circumstance. It was the kind of purity she preserved that moved me." The white woman as symbol of purity continues to dominate racist imaginations globally. In the United States, Hollywood continues to project this image, using it to affirm and reaffirm the power of white supremacy.

When people of color attempt to critically intervene and oppose white supremacy, particularly around the issue of representation, we are often dismissed as pushing narrow political correctness, or simply characterized as being no fun. Writing about cultural appropriation in *English is Broken Here* Coco Fusco explains: "The socialization I and many other affirmative action babies received to identify racism as the property only of ignorant, reactionary people, preferably from the past, functioned to deflect our attention from how whiteness operated in the present . . . To raise the specter of racism in the here and now, to suggest that despite their political beliefs and sexual preferences, white people operate within, and benefit from, white supremacist social structures is still tantamount to a declaration of war." When white supremacy is challenged and resisted, people of color and our allies in struggle risk the censorship that emerges when those who hold the power to dominate simply say to us, "You are extremist, you are the real racist, you are playing the race card." Of course the irony is that we are not actually allowed to play at the game of race, we are merely pawns in the hands of those who invent the games and determine the rules.

Every black person and person of color colludes with the existing system in small ways every day, even those among us who see ourselves as anti-racist radicals. This collusion happens simply because we are all products of the culture we live within and have all been subjected to the forms of socialization and acculturation that are deemed normal in our society. Through the cultivation of awareness, through the decolonization of our minds, we have the tools to break with the dominator model of human social engagement and the will to imagine new and different ways that people might come together. Martin Luther King, Jr. imagined a "beloved community," conceptualizing a world where people would bond on the basis of shared humanness. His vision remains. King taught that the

simple act of coming together would strengthen community.
Yet before he was assassinated he was beginning to see that
unlearning racism would require a change in both thinking
and action, and that people could agree to come together
across race but they would not make community.

Chris's
quote
purposed
educt.

To build community requires vigilant awareness of the work
we must continually do to undermine all the socialization that
leads us to behave in ways that perpetuate domination. A body
of critical theory is now available that explains all the workings
of white-supremacist thought and racism. But explanations
alone do not bring us to the practice of beloved community.
When we take the theory, the explanations, and apply them
concretely to our daily lives, to our experiences, we further and
deepen the practice of anti-racist transformation. Rather than
simply accept that class power often situates me in a world
where I have little or no contact with other black people, especially individuals from underprivileged classes, I as a black person with class privilege can actively seek out these relationships. More often than not to do this work I must make an
effort to expand my social world. In recent years, individual
white peers who have always seen themselves as anti-racist have
adopted children of color, only to realize (what should have
been apparent) that they did not really have intimate friend-
ships with people of color. They need to do their active
unlearning of white-supremacist thinking (which says you are
superior because of whiteness and therefore better able to
raise a non-white child than any colored person) by seeking to
forge relationships with people of color.

Time and time again I have observed white peers working
to unlearn white supremacy as they become aware of the reality that they have little contact with non-white people. They
open their "eyes" and see that there were always non-white
folks around them that they did not "see" when they were
blinded by white privilege stemming from racist foundations.
Time and time again I come to do anti-racist work at liberal

David Allen- Instructional curriculum is
the way we stratify

arts colleges that I am told are "all white" only to find that the majority of support staff and service workers are non-white. The presence of black people and/or people of color who are not seen as class peers is easily ignored in a context where the privileged identity is white. When we stop thinking and evaluating along the lines of hierarchy and can value rightly all members of a community we are breaking a culture of domination. White supremacy is easily reinscribed when individuals describe communities of students and faculty as "all white" rather than affirming diversity, even if it's evident only by the presence of a few individuals. Anti-racist work requires of all of us vigilance about the ways we use language. Either/or thinking is crucial to the maintenance of racism and other forms of group oppression. Whenever we think in terms of both/and we are better situated to do the work of community building.

Imagine the difference: on one campus I hear that white people remain the larger group but are made diverse by the presence of non-white individuals and that the majority wants to become diverse. On another campus, I hear that "we are all white," which negates the value of the presence of people of color, however few in number they may be. The language we use to express these ideas is usually awkward at first, but as we change to more inclusive language and normalize its use that awkwardness becomes less. Much of the white-supremacist thought and action we have all unconsciously learned surfaces in habitual behavior. Therefore it is that behavior we must become aware of and work to change. For example: black mothers frequently come to me to ask what they can do when their children come home from school saying they want to be "made white." Often these women will share that they have done everything to instill love of blackness. However, in every case the woman seeks to change her appearance to look lighter or to make her hair straighter.

In every case the individual resists the notion that the child "reads" her hypocrisy, that the child assumes that "if I cannot even be seen as beautiful, acceptable, worthy by my mother then that larger world that is telling me white is better every day must be right." This is a direct quote from a beautiful black female student in her early twenties who shared that this is what she used to tell herself. And as an adult when individuals would tell her how beautiful she is this is the message her inner voice would offer as a reminder. Even though many scholars and intellectuals mock the world of self-help, it is an important realm of self-recovery for the racially colonized mind. Speaking aloud daily affirmations to change long-imprinted, toxic messages is a useful strategy for cleansing the mind. It promotes vigilant awareness of the ways white-supremacist thinking (daily encoded in the world of advertisement, commercials, magazine images, etc.) enters our system and also empowers us to break its hold on our consciousness.

When I first chose to write books on the subject of love, I simply assumed that my audience would be interested readers of any race. Yet when I came to the table of decision-makers in the publishing world, I was asked to identify who the audience would be. It was explained to me that it might be difficult for me to attract "white readers" since I was associated with black liberation. I believed that I could transcend the race-based consumerism that is often the norm in our society. (If a movie has only white characters, it is presumed to be marketed in the direction of all consumers; it is for everybody. However if the movie has only black characters, it is perceived to be directed at a black market.) When I wrote *All about Love: New Visions*, I never identified my race in the book, though clearly the photo on the back showed my color, because I wanted to demonstrate by this gesture that black writers who write specifically on the subject of race are not always only interested in race. I wanted to show that we are all complex thinkers who can be both specific in our focus and universal. The either/or thinking that is at the heart of the white-supremacist–based Western metaphysical dualism teaches people they must choose to like either black images or white images, or see books by white people as written for everybody and books by black people for black people. The inclusive nature of both/and thinking allows us to be inclusive. As a child I never thought that Emily Dickinson wrote her poems just for white readers (and she was truly the first poet whose work I loved). When I later read the work of Langston Hughes I never though he was writing just for black readers. Both poets wrote about the world they knew most intimately.

As my awareness of the way white-supremacist thinking shapes even our choices of what books we read, what books we want to display on our coffee tables, intensified, I developed strategies of resistance. When my second book on love, *Salvation: Black People and Love*, looked specifically at the experiences of black folks, I had to challenge the use of the phrase "black love" by white and black readers. I had to make the point that I was talking about the same ideas of love I had written about in the first book (which no one called a book about white love) but now focusing on the impact those ways of thinking about love had made on the consciousness of black people. The assumption that "whiteness" encompasses that which is universal, and therefore for everybody, while "blackness" is specific, and therefore "for colored only," is white-supremacist thought. And yet many liberal people, along with their more conservative peers, think this way not because they are "bad" people or are consciously choosing to be racist but because they have unconsciously learned to think in this manner. Such thinking, like so many other thought patterns and actions that help perpetuate and maintain white supremacy, can be easily unlearned.

Thirty years of talking about racism and white supremacy, giving lectures and facilitating anti-racism workshops has shown me how easy it is for individuals to change their thoughts and actions when they become aware and when they desire to use that awareness to alter behavior. White-supremacist backlash, which has sought to undermine both the legacy of civil rights and the new focus on critical race theory and practice, continues to push the notion that racist thinking, particularly in white minds, cannot be changed. This is just simply not true. Yet this false assumption gained momentum because there has been no collective demonstration on the part of masses of white people that they are ready to end race-based domination, especially when it comes to the everyday manifestation of white-supremacist thinking, of white power.

Clearly, the most powerful indicator that white people wanted to see institutionalized racism end was the overall societal support for desegregation and integration. The fact that many white people did not link this support to ending everyday acts of white-supremacist thought and practice, however, has helped racism maintain its hold on our culture. To break that hold we need continual anti-racism activism. We need to generate greater cultural awareness of the way white-supremacist thinking operates in our daily lives. We need to hear from the individuals who know, because they have lived anti-racist lives, what everyone can do to decolonize their minds, to maintain awareness, change behavior, and create beloved community.

Teach 4

Democratic Education

Teachers who have a vision of democratic education assume that learning is never confined solely to an institutionalized classroom. Rather than embodying the conventional false assumption that the university setting is not the "real world" and teaching accordingly, the democratic educator breaks through the false construction of the corporate university as set apart from real life and seeks to re-envision schooling as always a part of our real world experience, and our real life. Embracing the concept of a democratic education we see teaching and learning as taking place constantly. We share the knowledge gleaned in classrooms beyond those settings thereby working to challenge the construction of certain forms of knowledge as always and only available to the elite.

When teachers support democratic education we automatically support widespread literacy. Ensuring literacy is the vital link between the public school system and university settings.

It is the public school that is the required schooling for everyone, that has the task of teaching students to read and write
and hopefully to engage in some form of critical thinking.
Everyone then who knows how to read and write has the tools
needed to access higher learning even if that learning cannot
and does not take place in a university setting. Our government mandates attendance at public school, thereby uphold-
ing public policy supporting democratic education. But the
politics of class elitism ensure that biases in the way knowledge
is taught often teach students in these settings that they are not
deemed sophisticated learners if they do not attend college.
This means that many students stop the practice of learning
because they feel learning is no longer relevant to their lives
once they graduate from high school unless they plan to
attend college. They have often learned in public school both
that college is not the "real" world and that the book learning
offered there has no relevance in the world outside university
walls. Even though all the knowledge coming from books in
colleges is accessible to any reader/thinker whether they
attend classes or not, tightly constructed class boundaries keep
most high school graduates who are not enrolled in colleges
from continued study. Even college students who receive
undergraduate degrees leave college settings to enter the
world of everyday work and tend to cease studying, basing their
actions on the false assumption that book-based learning has
little relevance in their new lives as workers. It is amazing how
many college graduates never read a book again once they
graduate. And if they read, they no longer study.

To bring a spirit of study to learning that takes place both
in and beyond classroom settings, learning must be understood as an experience that enriches life in its entirety. Quoting
from T. H. White's *The Once and Future King*, Parker Palmer
celebrates the wisdom Merlin the magician offers when he
declares: "The best thing for being sad is to learn something.
That is the only thing that never fails . . . Learn why the world

wags and what wags it. That is the only thing which the mind can never exhaust, never alienate, never be tortured by, never fear or distrust, and never dream of regretting. Learning is the thing for you." Parker adds to this declaration his own vital understanding that: "education at its best—this profound human transaction called teaching and learning—is not just about getting information or getting a job. Education is about healing and wholeness. It is about empowerment, liberation, transcendence, about renewing the vitality of life. It is about finding and claiming ourselves and our place in the world." Since our place in the world is constantly changing, we must be constantly learning to be fully present in the now. If we are not fully engaged in the present we get stuck in the past and our capacity to learn is diminished.

Educators who challenge themselves to teach beyond the classroom setting, to move into the world sharing knowledge, learn a diversity of styles to convey information. This is one of the most valuable skills any teacher can acquire. Through vigilant practice we learn to use the language that can speak to the heart of the matter in whatever teaching setting we may find ourselves in. When college professors who are democratic educators share knowledge outside the classroom, the work we do dispels the notion that academic workers are out of touch with a world outside the hallowed halls of academe. We do the work of opening up the space of learning so that it can be more inclusive, and challenge ourselves constantly to strengthen our teaching skills. These progressive practices are vital to maintaining democratic education, both in the classroom and out.

Authoritarian practices, promoted and encouraged by many institutions, undermines democratic education in the classroom. By undermining education as the practice of freedom, authoritarianism in the classroom dehumanizes and thus shuts down the "magic" that is always present when individuals are active learners. It takes the "fun out of study" and makes it repressive and oppressive. Authoritarian professors often invest in the notion that they are the only "serious" teachers, whereas democratic educators are often stereotyped by their more conservative counterparts as not as rigorous or as without standards. This is especially the case when the democratic educator attempts to create a spirit of joyful practice in the classroom. In *Pedagogy of the Heart*, Paulo Freire contends that democratic educators "must do everything to ensure an atmosphere in the classroom where teaching, learning, and studying are serious acts, but also ones that generate happiness." Explaining further he states: "Only to an authoritarian mind can the act of educating be seen as a dull task. Democratic educators can only see the acts of teaching, of learning, of studying as serious, demanding tasks that not only generate satisfaction but are pleasurable in and of themselves. The satisfaction with which they stand before the students, the confidence with which they speak, the openness with which they listen, and the justice with which they address the student's problems make the democratic educator a model. Their authority is affirmed without disrespect of freedom. . . . Because they respect freedom, they are respected." Democratic educators show by their habits of being that they do not engage in forms of socially acceptable psychological splitting wherein someone teaches only in the classroom and then acts as though knowledge is not meaningful in every other settings. When students are taught this, they can experience learning as a whole process rather than a restrictive practice that disconnects and alienates them from the world.

Conversation is the central location of pedagogy for the democratic educator. Talking to share information, to exchange ideas is the practice both inside and outside academic settings that affirms to listeners that learning can take place in varied time frames (we can share and learn a lot in five minutes) and that knowledge can be shared in diverse modes of speech. Whereas vernacular speech may seldom be used in the classroom by teachers it may be the preferred way to share knowledge in other settings. When educational settings become places that have as their central goal the teaching of bourgeois manners, vernacular speech and languages other than standard English are not valued. Indeed, they are blatantly devalued. While acknowledging the value of standard English the democratic educator also values diversity in language. Students who speak standard English, but for whom English is a second language, are strengthened in their bi-lingual self-esteem when their primary language is validated in the classroom. This valuation can occur as teachers incorporate teaching practices that honor diversity, resisting the conventional tendency to maintain dominator values in higher education.

Certainly as democratic educators we have to work to find ways to teach and share knowledge in a manner that does not reinforce existing structures of domination (those of race, gender, class, and religious hierarchies). Diversity in speech and presence can be fully appreciated as a resource enhancing any learning experience. In recent years we have all been challenged as educators to examine the ways in which we support, either consciously or unconsciously, existing structures of domination. And we have all been encouraged by democratic educators to become more aware, to make more conscious choices. We may unwittingly collude with structures of domination because of the way learning is organized in institutions. Or we may gather material to teach that is non-biased and yet present it in a manner that is biased, thus reinforcing existing oppressive hierarchies.

Without ongoing movements for social justice in our nation, progressive education becomes all the more important since it may be the only location where individuals can experience support for acquiring a critical consciousness, for any commitment to end domination. The two movements for social justice that have had the most transformative impact on our culture are anti-racist struggle and feminist movement. Understanding that the movement for activism often slows down once civil rights are won, both these movements worked to created locations for academic study precisely so that an unbiased approach to scholarship and learning would not only be legitimized in school and university settings, but would act as a catalyst to transform every academic discipline. Learning would then serve to educate students for the practice of freedom rather than the maintenance of existing structures of domination.

All the progressive study of race and gender taking place in university settings has had meaningful impact way beyond the academic classroom. Democratic educators who championed bringing an end to biased ways of teaching bridged the gap between the academic and the so called "real" world. Long before progressive scholars became interested in race or gender and diversity or multiculturalism, big business recognized the need to teach workers—particularly the deal makers, whose task was to create new markets around the world— about difference, about other cultures. Of course the foundation of this approach was not teaching to end domination but rather teaching to further the interests of the marketplace, but conservatives and liberals alike clearly recognized the necessity of teaching students in this nation perspectives that included a recognition of different ways of knowing. In the wake of this shift, generated by capitalist concerns to maintain power in a global marketplace, anti-racist and anti-sexist advocates were able to lobby successfully for challenging the ways imperialist notions of white supremacy, of nationalism, had created biases in educational material and in the teaching styles and strategies of educators.

Academic discourse, both written and spoken, on the subject of race and racism, on gender and feminism, made a major intervention, linking struggles for justice outside the academy with ways of knowing within the academy. This was really revolutionary. Educational institutions that had been founded on principles of exclusion—the assumption that the values that uphold and maintain imperialist white-supremacist capitalist patriarchy were truth, began to consider the reality of biases, and to discuss the value of inclusion. Yet many people supported inclusion only when diverse ways of knowing were taught as subordinate and inferior to the superior ways of knowing informed by Western metaphysical dualism and dominator culture. To counter this distorted approach to inclusion and diversity, democratic educators have stressed the value of pluralism. In the essay "Commitment and Openness: A Contemplative Approach to Pluralism," Judith Simmer-Brown explains: "pluralism is not diversity. Diversity is a fact of modern life—especially in America. There are tremendous differences in our communities—ethnically, racially, religiously. Diversity suggests the fact of such differences. Pluralism, on the other hand, is a response to the fact of diversity. In pluralism, we commit to engage with the other person or the other community. Pluralism is a commitment to communicate with and relate to the larger world—with a very different neighbor, or a distant community." Many educators embrace the notion of diversity while resisting pluralism or any other thinking that suggests that they should no longer uphold dominator culture.

Affirmative action was aimed at creating greater diversity and it was, at least in theory, a positive practice of reparations, providing access to those groups who had previously been denied education and other rights because of group-based oppression. Despite its many flaws, affirmative action successfully broke barriers to gender and racial inclusion, benefitting white women especially. As our schools became more diverse, professors were often challenged to the core of their being. Old ideas of studying and learning other people's work in order to find our own theories and defend them were and are being constantly challenged. Judith Simmer-Brown offers the useful insight that this mode of learning does not allow us to embrace ambiguity and uncertainty. She contends: "As educators, one of the best things that we can do for our students is to not force them into holding theories and solid concepts but rather to actually encourage the process, the inquiry involved, and the times of not knowing—with all of the uncertainties that go along with that. This is really what supports going deep. This is openness." While I was working with professors at a leading liberal arts college to help them unlearn dominator models of education, I heard white males voice their feelings of fear and uncertainty about giving up models they knew. The males were willing to accept the challenge to transform and yet were fearful because they simply did not know what would be the source of their power if they were no longer relying on a racialized gendered notion of authority to maintain that power. Their honesty helped all of us imagine and articulate what the positive outcomes of a pluralist approach to learning might be.

One of the most positive outcomes is a commitment to "radical openness," the will to explore different perspectives and change one's mind as new information is presented. Throughout my career as a democratic educator I have known many brilliant students who seek education, who dream of service in the cause of freedom, who despair or become fundamentally dismayed because colleges and universities are structured in ways that dehumanize, that lead them away from the spirit of community in which they long to live their lives. More often than not, these students, especially gifted students of color from diverse class backgrounds, give up hope. They do poorly in their studies. They take on the mantle of victimhood. They fail. They drop out. Most of them have had no guides to teach them how to find their way in educational systems that, though structured to maintain domination, are not closed systems and therefore have within them subcultures of resistance where education as the practice of freedom still happens. Way too many gifted students never find these subcultures, never encounter the democratic educators who could help them find their way. They lose heart.

For more than thirty years I have witnessed students who do not want to be educated to be oppressors come close to graduation—and then sabotage themselves. They are the students who turn away from school with just one semester or one course to finish before they graduate. Sometimes they are brilliant graduate students who just never write their dissertations. Afraid that they will not be able to keep the faith, to become democratic educators, afraid that they will enter the system and *become* it, they turn away. Competitive education rarely works for students who have been socialized to value working for the good of the community. It rends them, tearing them apart. They experience levels of disconnection and fragmentation that destroy all pleasure in learning. These are the students who most need the guiding influence of democratic educators.

Forging a learning community that values wholeness over division, disassociation, splitting, the democratic educator works to create closeness. Palmer calls it the "intimacy that does not annihilate difference." As a student who came to undergraduate and graduate education by way of the radical movements for social justice that had opened space that had been closed, I learned to take community where I found it, bonding across race, gender, class, religious experience in order to save and protect the part of myself that wanted to stay in an academic world, that wanted to choose an intellectual life. The bonds I forged were with the individuals who, like myself, valued learning as an end itself and not as a means to reach another end, class mobility, power, status. We were the folks who knew that whether we were in an academic setting or not, we would continue to study, to learn, to educate.

Teach 5

What Happens When
White People Change

Pinpointing that particular historical moment in anti-racist struggle when black people begin to endorse the notion that all white people were racist and were unable to change is difficult. In his autobiography *Walking with the Wind*, civil rights activist John Lewis sees that moment as beginning with electoral politics, when the Mississippi Freedom Democratic Party was denied representation in the seats of governmental power. Lewis remembers: "As far as I'm concerned, this was the turning point of the civil rights movement. I'm absolutely convinced of that. Until then, despite every setback and disappointment and obstacle we faced over the years, the belief still prevailed that the system would work, the system would listen, the system would respond. Now, for the first time, we had made our way to the center of the system. We had played by the rules, done everything we were supposed to do, had played the game exactly as required, had arrived at the doorstep and found the door slammed in our face." Racial integration ushered in a world where many black folks played by the rules only to face the reality that white racism was not changing, that the system of white supremacy remained intact even as it allowed black people greater access. To many black people who had dreamed the dream, who had believed that racism could be changed by law and interaction, this was cause for despair. In their eyes, racist white people were betraying democracy, contemptuously making light of the oppression and pain black people had suffered.

Growing up in the world of racial apartheid, I had always known that there were courageous individual white people who sacrificed power, status, and privilege to be anti-racist. I heard their voices as they sat in my grandmother's house on the white side of town and gave voice to their beliefs in justice. I saw them cross the boundaries at a time when they risked life and limb to do so. In my childhood I knew that white people could change. And yet I knew that most white people did not want to change; that hurt, the knowledge that white people embraced racial domination as their privilege and their right. Racist white people were the norm. The white people who fascinated me, the white people I wanted to know, then and now, were the rare white folks who had the courage to choose against racism, to choose and to change. In the world I grew up in, a white person who dared to cross the boundaries and be actively anti-racist was respected by black people.

Militant anti-racist struggle spearheaded by patriarchal black people (mostly men) ushered in the idea of white folks as always and only the enemy. There are fundamental differences in the civil rights Southern-based anti-racist struggle and the Northern- and West Coast–based militant black struggle. Southern-based anti-racist struggle always pushed the notion that we are all one, that the goal of ending racial domination was more than just the gaining of civil rights, the ending of discrimination; it was also a vision of diverse people living together in peace. Militant black power rejected this vision of beloved community and invested in a vision of white folks as always and only racist; they were the enemy. Even if they were doing the work of justice they were still deemed the enemy because of the fact of whiteness. In a reversal of the racist thinking that condemned black folks on the basis skin color, nationalist militant patriarchal black power movement condemned all whites on the basis of skin color, not on the basis of beliefs and behaviors.

Even though the vast majority of African-Americans did not support the ideology of national militant patriarchal black power movement, the notion that white people were the enemy gained validity as black people, particularly our leaders, were assassinated and state terrorism stifled militant black protest. When integration failed to rid the nation of racism, many black people despaired and the notion that white folks were racists, that they were not willing to change, gained greater momentum. Rather than focusing on the individual heroic struggles of white folks who committed themselves to anti-racist justice, many black folks dismissed their effort as though it could have no real transformative meaning given the collective world of white racism. This thinking combined with the cynicism among whites about challenging and changing racism fundamentally undermines anti-racist struggle in our nation. The black people/people of color who truly believe that white people cannot change can only embrace the logic of victimhood. They are the doomsayers investing in the belief that there is no way out.

No one is born a racist. Everyone makes a choice. Many of us made the choice in childhood. A white child taught that hurting others is wrong, who then witnesses racial assaults on black people, who questions that and then is told by adults that this hurting is acceptable because of their skin color, then makes a moral choice to collude or to oppose. A large majority of the white people I knew in the apartheid South who put their lives on the line to choose being anti-racist made that choice in childhood. Ann, one of the few white females in my high school in the late sixties who offered real friendship, was consistently anti-racist. We are still friends today, more than thirty years after we first met. She says that she made her choice as a child. To Ann, it was a moral choice stemming from all that she had learned about right and wrong. It was a choice for justice.

Ann was able to maintain the integrity of her choice as a teenager in part because her parents did not attempt to impose white-supremacist values on her. Working in the tobacco industry, her father encountered black and white folks, as did her mother in the health industry. They taught her that, as she put it, "there is good and bad among all races." When I interviewed her for this book Ann remembered that her father never opposed her crossing the boundaries of race to build friendship, to build community. He never warned her about the risk she was taking. But he did tell her that other white folks where watching and were not happy with her behavior. Ann remembers her father conveying the message sent by an aunt that she should not be opposing white supremacy. Her response was to tell her dad that her aunt "should mind her own business."

Ann did not have relational contact with black people until high school, but she had made her choice in her younger years. When she made black friends at school, she wanted to bring them home to spend the night. And even though her parents let her know that would not be a good idea they did not demand of her any form of racial allegiance. The anti-racist values Ann embraced have stayed with her throughout her life. Being anti-racist feels as simple and as natural to her as breathing. The world we grew up in has changed little when it comes to race. Segregation is still the norm in social relationships. Ann is still crossing the tracks. And when white folks warn of the dangers, she just laughs knowingly. Confident that there are good and bad in every group, she seeks the good. That seeking has stood her in good stead.

In my memoir *Wounds of Passion*, I wrote about our mutual high school friend Ken a white male who also dared to cross the boundaries of race. Unlike Ann's parents Ken's folks were consciously committed to social justice. His dad was one of the white ministers in our town who openly opposed racism and white supremacy. When I did readings from *Wounds of Passion*, especially the passages about our struggle to be friends in a social context of racial apartheid, audiences would invariably ask about Ken. We had lost touch for a long while and reunited at the first racially integrated high school reunion, the twentieth. When I was called to see if I would come, my first question was "would Ken be there." A former white male classmate who was doing the calling chuckled and replied that he had just spoken to Ken, whose first response had been to ask if I would be there. Ken and I reunited. We have been close ever since. I moved to the Florida city where he and his wife lived, moved around the corner, bringing blackness to their predominantly white neighborhood. Ken is politically anti-racist, but his social life is still mostly white. He cheerfully absorbs my critiques, even my disappointment that he is not as radical as he was when we were teenagers.

Like many white liberals, Ken sees the "whiteness" of his social life as more an accident of circumstance than a choice. He would welcome greater diversity in the neighborhood. However, he does not consciously do enough work either in his own social life or in the larger community to make that diversity possible.

As allies in anti-racist struggle, Ken and Ann made sacrifices. The bonds of communion and community we forged in resisting white supremacy connect us today. Those bonds are much stronger than the ties I have with most of my white academic peers who write about race and racism but who do not allow anti-racist action to govern how they live their lives.

Words are inadequate when we try to evoke the experience of little children in a Southern, white-supremacist culture where state-sanctioned racial terrorism kept everyone in their place. The Jim Crow South was our South Africa. Desegregation did not bring social racial integration. Mingling, crossing the boundaries of race was still a question of individual choice. Most white folks continued to believe in white supremacy and lived their lives accordingly.

Ironically, de-segregation and racial integration was viewed by liberals and conservatives as the action that would bring the races together. In reality even when black and white came together, they were still separated by white-supremacist beliefs. Racism maintained segregation in the minds and hearts of white people even when it ended legally. Given that reality, white people who choose to be actively anti-racist are heroic. And their heroism goes unnoticed in a world where the overall assumption is that all white people are racist and they cannot or will not change. Dangerous and detrimental, this thinking maintains and reinforces white supremacy.

While it is a truism that every citizen of this nation, white or colored, is born into a racist society that attempts to socialize us from the moment of our birth to accept the tenets of white supremacy, it is equally true that we can choose to resist this socialization. Children do this every day. Babies who stare with wonder and bliss at caretakers, not caring whether they are white or colored, are already actively resisting racist socialization. Whether or not any of us become racists is a choice we make. And we are called to choose again and again where we stand on the issue of racism at different moments in our lives. This has been especially the case for white people. Few white people make the choice to be fundamentally anti-racist and consistently live the meaning of this choice. These are the white folks who know intimately by heart the truth that racism is not in their blood, that it is always about consciousness. And where there is consciousness there is choice. In *Pedagogy of the*

Heart, Paulo Freire reminds us that racism is not inherent declaring: "We are not racist; we become racist just as we may stop being that way."

If we fail to acknowledge the value and significance of individual anti-racist white people we not only diminish the work they have done and do to transform their thinking and behavior, but we prevent other white people from learning by their example. All people of color who suffer racial exploitation and oppression know that white supremacy will not end until racist white people change. Anyone who denies that this change can happen, that one can move from being racist to being actively anti-racist is acting in collusion with the existing forces of racial domination.

Maybe I would have despaired about the capacity of white people to become anti-racist if I had not witnessed firsthand individual Southern white folks (older people), born and bred in a culture of white supremacy, resist it, choosing anti-racism and a love of justice. These were folks who made their choices in circumstances of great danger, in the midst of racial warfare. To honor their commitment rightly we have to fully accept their transformation. To ask folks to change, to surrender their allegiance to white supremacy, then to mock them by saying that they can never be free of racist thinking is an abomination. If white folks can never be free of white-supremacist thought and action, then black folks/colored folks can never be free. It is as simple as that. We must accept that black folks/people of color are as socialized to embrace white-supremacist thinking and behavior as our white counterparts. If we can resist, if we can refuse to embrace racist thinking and action, so can they.

Leaving the South to attend a predominantly white liberal arts college on the West Coast, I entered a world where it was fashionable to mouth anti-racist sentiments without truly undergoing the radical transformation in thought and action that must also take place. Active in feminist movement on campus I was stunned by the extent to which white female peers were ignorant of race, racism, and white female privilege. When you grow up in a world of racial apartheid where all manner of terrorizing assaults are used to keep white and black in their "proper" place, white and black folks know intimately that race matters and they know the privileges accorded the white race via the institutionalization of white supremacy.

During my undergraduate years at Stanford University I met groups of liberal well-meaning white folks who were in theory anti-racist, but the vast majority of them had little or no actual everyday contact with black people. Many people forget that the apartheid South did not keep white and black folks apart in daily life but rather enforced subordination and domination through a system of manners and "proper" decorum while allowing close contact. As a consequence, many Southern white folks who had been waited upon all their lives, from birth until death, by black caregivers never had the fear of black presence that Northerners or folks on the West Coast had. And even though I entered Stanford in the early part of the seventies, at a time when racial integration had challenged and changed racial discrimination, the South was slow to change.

When I became an academic focusing my work on feminist theory I, along with other individual radical women of color, challenged white women who spoke of sisterhood to unlearn their racism, to take the time to revise the theories that they were creating from a perspective of racial biases. This intervention exposed the racism of most white feminist activists, but it also revealed and highlighted those individual white women who either were already committed to anti-racist being, or who were in the process of allowing their lives to be changed through understanding the intersections of racism and sexism. While I was one of the keenest critics of the way racism informed much feminist theory and practice, I have also continually celebrated those individual white women who are true comrades and sisters—women who are anti-racist.

Often I am asked to explain why I could, can, and do critique the racism of white women within feminist movement and in our society as a whole and yet maintain deep bonds of solidarity, care, and love with individual white women. My explanation is rooted in the recognition and praise of the individual anti-racist white women I encountered and encounter in feminist movement who are utterly and steadfastly committed to eradicating racism, to racial justice. As comrades in struggle, the presence and actions of these individual white women renew my faith in the power of white people to resist racism. I feel this especially during times when I am discouraged about the more widespread white female passive acceptance of racism.

In the academic world I found those women in colleagues like Zillah Eisenstein. More than twenty years ago I met Zillah while speaking on a panel about feminist theory. Since we are both fond of spirited dialectical exchange we debated, argued, and in our own way fell in comradely love. When I told her that I felt she had used my work without really giving me credit, she did not respond with the defensiveness and fear I often encountered whenever I challenged white women. Confident, she stated she would go back, take a look at the work and if she agreed with me make amends. This encounter was so refreshing. We regarded each other as equals, as peers. I had become so weary of encountering white people, especially white women, who used fear as a practice of dehumanization. The same white female colleagues who would engage in professional debate with white female peers would often engage me as though they were Jane in the jungle threatened by a raging beast. Their irrational, racialized fear separated us.

Of course as Zillah became a lifelong political comrade and personal friend, I learned that she was born into a household of serious Jewish political activists who were fundamentally anti-racist. Living among black folks and working with them, her parents embodied the truth that we are created equal. Zillah has done to same for her daughter. The choices Zillah's parents made to be anti-racist caused difficulty in their lives, and yet they never wavered. Zillah has herself become someone who does not waver in her resistance to imperialist white-supremacist capitalist patriarchal domination. Early on I learned the phrase "capitalist patriarchy" from reading Zillah's work.

Accepting Zillah and other white women comrades as anti-racist in their being does not mean that I or they ignore the reality that we can all be as anti-racist as we want to be and still make mistakes. There are individual women of color who work with Zillah yet who do not see as her as I do. I can only say that they do not know her as I know her. Once I came to talk at her college, and with bold zeal she wanted to introduce me, but the women of color who were my hosts felt that "like the typical white woman she was trying to take over." Talking with them I could see that they brought to this encounter a pent up impatience and rage at white female racism that was not simply about Zillah's action. I understood their rage even though I did not share their interpretation. Realizing that something was "wrong," Zillah was both hurt and disturbed. Like any of us who take courageous stands against racism it was hard to accept being lumped, even if just for a moment, with all the unenlightened white folks who have no intention of unlearning their racism.

Engaged in critical dialogue about this encounter, Zillah and I were painfully reminded of the damage white supremacy has done to our capacity as women to trust one another. Most black women encounter racism from white women. That remembered assault may leave us feeling guarded, feeling we cannot allow ourselves to trust any white woman. On the flip side, white women who seek to be our comrades may work overtime to show us that they are worthy, but in a manner that is ultimately patronizing. Anytime we strive to prove our worth by exaggerated gestures there is usually an underlying problem of low self-esteem.

Relationships between black and white women are often charged by the dynamics of competition. Whether or not that competition stems from a racialized base, it will ultimately manifest itself in a racialized response. Sexism pits women against one another, and the power struggle that ensues may become even more intense when racial difference is added to the mix. Anti-racist white women are not afraid to engage with critiques by black women/women of color because those white women fundamentally understand that as long as we fear facing our differences and avoid conflict we cannot arrive at a true place of solidarity and sisterhood.

When black people/people of color fully embrace the reality that white people who choose to do so can be anti-racist to the core of their being then we draw these folks to us. Their commitment to anti-racism does not mean they never make mistakes, that they never buy into race privilege, or that they never enact in daily life racial domination. This could always happen on an unconscious level. What it does mean is that when they make a mistake they are able to face it and make needed repair.

Since I believe wholeheartedly that white people can choose to be anti-racist, I look for those individuals in every walk of life who have made this choice. The publishing world has little diversity, and is way behind the small progress made in educational settings. But I have found those rare white folks who understood, who are anti-racist. When I interviewed Lisa Holton, a high-level executive at Disney Hyperion Children's Books who has worked hard to further publishing books by and about people of color, I asked where her commitment to racial justice was made. She shared that she was the child of a divorced couple at a time when it was not common, that she had been an "outsider" in school eating her lunch with three other outsiders, two of whom were black, and all of whom were the children of divorced parents. It was in that setting that she forged her bonds across the boundaries of race and made her choice to be anti-racist. She recalls: "I just really saw what racism does to everybody." Awareness of the pain racial injustice causes in the everyday lives of black folks was the catalyst that led her to reject white supremacy. When I talk with black folks she supervises they just express such joy that they can work with a white person "who never lords it over" them. The "it" she could use to maintain hierarchal domination is racial privilege.

Often the white women I have encountered who are most passionate in their will to be anti-racist, who carry their commitment from theory to practice, are gay women. Interviewing them I heard again and again that discrimination against them on the basis of sexuality helped bridge their understanding of the pain of race-based discrimination. Rather than assuming that this pain was identical to the pain they experienced, they accepted the "bridge" as merely a base to walk across, allowing them to learn from people of color the nature of our experience in the social context of white supremacy.

Many white gay people are unable to bridge the gap. They remain unable to look at the way in which whiteness and white power give them access to privilege to the role of dominator. They refuse to see the ways discrimination can impact on our consciousness differently even though the forms it takes are the same. Often gay white people look down on black people because they perceive us to be more homophobic or less sexually progressive. These stereotyped assumptions are rooted in white-supremacist thinking, which deems white folks to be always more sophisticated and complex than people of color. White gay women and men who are fundamentally anti-racist do not need to use the notion that they are intellectually superior or to legitimize their fear of us.

Writing openly and honestly about these issues in her collection of "lesbian essays on Southern culture," Mab Segrest describes the pain she feels when she acknowledges the power of white supremacy. When "as a white person—I realize what white people have done and are doing in the world, the more I am tempted by the tragic voice which tells me . . . It is too late." Humor is the vehicle Segrest uses to restore her spirit: "My comic sense. . . . encourages my white self not to hate itself since I can change. For white women doing anti-racist work, one of our chief challenges is to find ways of overcoming our feelings of self-hatred and despair brought about by an increased knowledge of our white heritage. The sense of humor is also the sense of faith and trust and hope." Humor is vital to our efforts to bond across race. Laughing together intervenes in our fear of making mistakes.

A group of white women, mostly gay, who have worked to create in their collectively owned bookstore an atmosphere of beloved communities that embraces everyone, are the owners and workers of Charis bookstore in Atlanta. To eliminate the racial tension/fear that could arise when people of color enter what is often a predominantly white setting, these women practice a basic civility to all. Years ago we/people of color would often complain that we would enter feminist bookstores and be treated as though we do not belong. Embracing civility in interactions across race can serve as a simple way to break down barriers created by white-supremacist thought and action. In the world I grew up in, black people's subservience was measured by the degree to which we extended ourselves to be courteous and civil to whites; now, anti-racist white people use the practice of civility as a strategy of resistance.

The principles that govern interaction between black and women folks in a white-supremacist society, that help us resist and form solidarity, need to be identified. One principle is the will to form a conscious, cooperative partnership that is rooted in mutuality. Striving to be mutual is the principle that best mediates situations where there is unequal status. Of course, we cannot forge boundaries across the barriers that racism creates if we want always to be safe or to avoid conflict. In feminist settings, during my first year of college, I was always confused

Striving to be mutual.

when my peers would encourage us to participate in activist revolution on the one hand, and then on the other hand stress the importance of safety. The emphasis on safety in feminist settings often served as a barrier to cross-racial solidarity because these encounters did not feel "safe" and were often charged with tension and conflict. Working with white students on unlearning racism, one of the principles we strive to embody is the value of risk, honoring the fact that we may learn and grow in circumstances where we do not feel safe, that the presence of conflict is not necessarily negative but rather its meaning is determined by how we cope with that conflict. Trusting our ability to cope in situations where racialized conflict arises is far more fruitful than insisting on safety as always the best or only basis for bonding.

Individual white men working to be, like their white female counterparts, fully anti-racist, rarely get the attention white folks who are actively racists get. When any white male in our government makes a racist statement he receives a hundred times more attention than the lone white male who publicly stands against racist policies. Through the years I have noticed that people of color who are still invested in power struggles judge anti-racist white folks much more harshly than their racist counterparts. Often the anti-racist white person must endure social isolation, rejected by racist white folks and by people of color who may either fear being betrayed or who may simply be enacting dominator power via exclusion.

Art professor Mark Johnson, a white male who knows what it feels like to be the object of scorn or ridicule from both sides of the fence, white folks who think he is "too pro black" and black folks who seem him a being the uppity white male. It is vital that we refuse to allow rejection by any group to change one's commitment to anti-racism. Love of justice cannot be sustained if it is only a manipulation to be with the in-crowd, whoever they may be. Many white folks worked for civil rights, then passively dropped the struggle when critiqued by people of color or told by them they were not wanted. Anti-racist white folks recognize that their ongoing resistance to white supremacism is genuine when it is not determined in any way by the approval or disapproval of people of color. This does not mean that they do not listen and learn from critique, but rather that they understand fully that their choice to be anti-racist must be constant and sustained to give truth to the reality that racism can end.

Mark believes that service is central to anti-racist commitment. People of color, myself included, trust him because we see the work he does on behalf of ending white supremacy, work for which he receives no visible reward. To him the reward is knowing that he is living a life of integrity, living the truth of his commitment to ending racism, within and without. His work on behalf of racial justice has brought to him a beloved community where diversity is a given. When I hear white people complain about not being able to make the social contact they would like to have with people of color, my response is always to encourage them to work actively for racial justice, because that work will draw to them the community they desire, if their longing is sincere and not an excuse for living a life cloaked in unchanged whiteness.

There are so many individuals I could name whose lives bear witness to the power of anti-racist white people, folks like longtime activist Grace Lee Boggs, that it would take pages and pages to share their stories. These pages should be written. Everyone should hear their testimony.

Activist, writer, lesbian Barbara Deming transformed her life by refusing to support white supremacy. Working in the South during the civil rights movement she was, by her power as an individual, working for justice. She learned firsthand that "the individual can act" and that actions on behalf of social change "has weight." Like Deming, I have learned firsthand that individual white people who choose to be anti-racist make a difference. Speaking of her work with black people during dangerous times wherein she risked arrest, Deming writes that she finds joy in struggle, community, and a courage to resist that left her proclaiming "I am no longer the same." All white people who choose to be anti-racist proclaim this truth. Challenging racism, white supremacy, they are transformed. Free of the will to dominate on the basis of race, they can bond with people of color in beloved community living the truth of our essential humanness.

Teach 6

Standards

Throughout the United States segregated schools are becoming more the norm. As class mobility and a racist real estate market make predominantly white neighborhoods more common, especially in areas where new expensive homes are constructed, schools are being built to meet the needs of these neighborhoods, inner-city schools or schools in small cities or towns close to downtown areas tend to be the ones that have ethnic diversity. Many are predominantly black, Hispanic, *or* ~~are composed of a non-white ethnic mixture. This ipso facto~~ *Because of* racial segregation is usually seen as having nothing to do with *the so-* institutionalized racism but rather is deemed more a class issue. The old racial segregation in education is being re-inscribed, complete with schools deemed inferior that are composed of our nation's non-white poor and working class; those schools receive less funding and, as a consequence, lack resources for needed supplies. And yet individual African-

Americans are more inclined than ever to support segregated schools because they fear the racist biases that shape curriculum, and the perspectives of unenlightened racist teachers of all colors, in public schools.

Having attended segregated schools in the apartheid South until my junior high school years, I can testify to the fact that these school years supported the foundation of healthy self-esteem as regards education. Born in the fifties, I was raised in a segregated world where education was glorified; it was held up as a means for both self-advancement and racial uplift. In those segregated schools it was clear that there were some students who excelled in their studies and some who did not. It was simply assumed that being black and being smart in book-learning were compatible. All the smart book-learning people we knew were black: our French and German teachers, our physics and chemistry teachers and so on. Yet even in the world of the segregated school, a gap separated smart students from those students who did not wish to learn. As in all schools, irrespective of race, smart students were often ridiculed, seen as geeks or nerds. Even though my parents encouraged me, wanted me to be smart, they also joked about my always having my head in a book. They were afraid that too much book-learning made one weird if it was not balanced with social engagement. Irrespective of race, the parents I know, especially those with gifted children who would rather study than go outside and play, often express the same fear that my parents had, the fear that too much studying can lead to social alienation. Of course there was never any notion that too much studying made me, or anyone else I knew, less black. Indeed, my parents longed for me to attend a historically black college so that I would continue to learn from smart black thinkers.

Certainly, when the schools were desegregated, all black children in our town rode buses that took us into white neighborhoods and into white schools. Almost all the teachers in those schools were white. Gifted academic classes filled with hard-working black students no longer existed; instead a few of us were selected to be integrated into the all-white gifted classes. More often than not black girls were chosen over black boys (despite desegregation, the racist fear of contact between black males and white females still dictated that these two groups be kept apart). Black supporters of the civil rights struggle for desegregation of schools did not take into account the way our self-esteem as black students would be affected when we were taught by racist teachers. In my family we were encouraged to ignore the racism (not let it upset us) and to focus on our studies. Yet it was obvious to every black student in these predominantly white schools that our teachers did not really believe we were as capable of learning as white children did. Smart black students were deemed exceptional. We were often viewed as "freaks of nature" by racist teachers and by those rare, caring white teachers who were nonetheless influenced by the white-supremacist idea that black folks were never as smart as white folks.

Black schools were locations where our self-esteem as black students was affirmed. This was not because all our teachers were black, but because the majority of them were politically astute about the impact of racist thinking on black self-esteem and chose to counter that. In truth, there were some black teachers who were as white-supremacist in their thinking about the nature of intelligence as their white counterparts. But they were in the minority. If segregated schools became the norm today, it would not follow that the vast majority of black teachers would have critical consciousness about race, because education in predominantly white racist environments has socialized a huge body of African-American teachers to passively accept white-supremacist thinking about intelligence. Black children taught by black teachers who believe they are not capable of academic excellence are no better off than black children taught by white teachers who see them as academically sub-standard.

To support segregated schools in the hopes that they will, as in the far too distant past, be places where healthy self-esteem might be affirmed would be a gesture of despair. Ultimately, it would lead to the further isolation of black students from ways of knowing and learning that are needed for useful citizenship in a global community. Many educators are concerned with the fact that, across class, black children often behave as though book-learning and being smart in school makes them "less black identified." Rarely do these educators acknowledge that equating education with whiteness is a way of thinking that most black folks acquired in predominantly white school systems. Black students who mock their studious black peers have themselves been socialized via schools and mass media to believe that education has no positive meaning in their lives and that too much education will lead them away from "blackness." In contemporary school settings, where teachers are racially mixed and students are predominantly if not all black, negative attitudes about education can still abound. White-supremacist thinking, and the internalized self-hatred it promotes, may lead unenlightened teachers, even individual black teachers, to teach as though black students are academically less capable of excellence.

Such thinking is not simply rampant in the public schools; it abounds in colleges and universities. Often when individual black students realize that teachers and peers in predominantly white settings view them as less capable, they begin to perform in ways that make for "confirmation bias," that is, if a teacher acts as though a black student is unable to perform, well the student will perform poorly thus satisfying the teacher's expectations. If black students find that despite their efforts to excel they receive poor grades irrespective of the quality of their work, they may choose to turn in work that is sub-standard.

Awareness of the ways white-supremacist thinking permeates our culture despite gains in civil rights has helped concerned educators of all races recognize the importance of working to unlearn racism. This is the work that prepares all of us to teach in ways that educate for the practice of freedom. Academics, especially college teachers and professors, who have dared to examine the way in which white supremacy shapes our thinking, in both what we teach and how we teach, have created a small, revolutionary subculture within the educational system in our nation. Many of these academics teach and do scholarship in the area of Ethnic Studies, Women's Studies, and Cultural Studies. I began to sharpen my critical thinking about the nature of race and gender in Women's Studies classes. The critiques of race and racism that emerged in feminist settings changed the nature of feminist scholarship. More than any other movement for social justice in our society, feminist movement has been exemplary in promoting forms of critique that challenge white-supremacist thought on the level of theory and practice. The momentum established in feminist movement served as a catalyst for the progressive work on race and racism that emerged and continues to emerge in Cultural Studies.

Despite the continued prevalence of racism, of white-supremacist thought and action, academic settings are one of the few locations in our nation where individuals cross the boundaries of race to learn from one another and join in fellowship together. Much anti-feminist backlash, in particular the attack on Women's Studies, like the attack on Black/Ethnic Studies, emerged not because these programs were failing to educate but rather *because* they were successfully educating students to be critical thinkers. These programs helped, and help, many students shift their ideas about learning from passively embracing education as a means of joining a professional managerial class to thinking about education as the practice of freedom. Rather than punishing students for interrogating the forms of knowledge offered them, they encouraged them to repudiate educational practices that reinforce dominant ideol-

ogy, to open their minds and think critically. They learned to
think in ways that reinforce self-determination.

Education as the practice of freedom affirms healthy self-
esteem in students as it promotes their capacity to be aware
and live consciously. It teaches them to reflect and act in ways
that further self-actualization, rather than conformity to the
status quo. Professors like myself, who entered colleges because
of affirmative action programs, who did not come from middle-
class backgrounds, who were often the first in our families to
attend college, were uniquely situated to embrace alternative
modes of thinking during our student years. Entering the academic world as assistant professors, we were brought face to
face with a corporate-based educational system that rewarded
obedience to the status quo rather than radical approaches to
teaching and learning. As a graduate student I relied on radical sub-cultures within the academy to sustain me. Those subcultures were harder to find as a professor. Hard to find but
not impossible.

Feminist Studies, African-American Studies and Cultural
Studies are the locations within the academic world where I
have found individual colleagues with whom I have felt intellectual and political resonance. Then there has been the rare
administrator who, though conservative in outlook, has
offered support from a space of radical openness. Often democratic educators find ourselves on the margins of the academic mainstream. Our presence may constitute a threat to
the very individuals we might have imagined would be the colleagues with whom we might most likely bond. Throughout my
academic career I have been given support by rare individual
white males, usually administrators. When I first gave a lecture
at Oberlin College, where there was a position for an associate
professor in my field, a Southern-born white male dean called
to offer me the position. In his Southern twang he joked with
me: "If I don't hire you I will lose my job—what did you do to
students here?" Labeled a racist sexist man by most of the fem-

inist faculty, this dean and I connected in part because of the respect he showed me based on his understanding of the racism in Southern education. As a white Southerner he, unlike most of the white feminist colleagues, had intimate knowledge of how arduous my journey to the world of academe had been. He recalls: "I certainly did have the sense that you had deep strength, that it took that to get from where you started to where you are." Unlike many of the white female colleagues, he was not threatened by that strength; he admired it.

While I agreed with my colleagues that he often acted in ways that helped maintain racist and sexist hierarchies (but at times so did they), I also saw that he could at times act in the interest of justice and fair play. To me it was vital to encourage and support that part of him that was not conventional or closed. The more I supported him when he acted outside the box, sometimes making decisions that were quite radical, the more I was able to see and work with him as a potential ally rather than an enemy. I approached him in much of the same spirit of radical openness that I used in the classroom. To successfully do the work of unlearning domination, a democratic educator has to cultivate a spirit of hopefulness about the capacity of individuals to change.

Often groups subordinated by any form of group oppression—be it race, gender, class, or religion—will seek to form community with those like themselves by bonding on the basis of shared negative beliefs and understandings about oppressors. Together they will reinforce the "power" of those who dominate, even as they identify ways dominator culture keeps them down. By investing in the notion that they can only be "victims" in relation to those who have power over them, who may more often than not deploy that power in a way that reinforces oppressive hierarchy, they lose sight not only of their strength to resist but of the possibility that they can intervene and change the perspective of those in power. Once feminist professors decide a male colleague is sexist and refuse to see any glimmer of positive action on his part that could be the catalyst for change, they collude in keeping oppressive systems intact. Similarly, when non-white professors insist that white colleagues are always and only capable of acting as racists, they collude in reinforcing the notion that dominator culture is an absolute system, that it cannot be changed.

As I spent time with the white male dean deemed racist and sexist, I found that he was quite willing to share information with me, nurturing my academic development. He helped me understand how the system worked, acting at times as a mentor. Dominant groups often maintain their power by keeping information from subordinate groups. That dominance is altered when knowledge is shared in a way that reinforces mutual partnership. When I would talk to colleagues who "hated" this dean, suggesting that he was open to change, more often than not I would receive the feedback that he was just attracted to me, that he liked me, that his interaction with me was just a "special" case. When I asked him if he thought our interaction was "unique," he identified the "click" between us as a combination of personal resonance and professional admiration. Even so, this would still be an opening in a system that often appears closed. If we are not able to find and enter the open spaces in closed systems (no matter the catalyst for the openness), we doom ourselves by reinforcing the belief that these educational systems cannot be changed.

Throughout my academic career I have sought the spaces of openness, fixing my attention less on the ways colleagues are closed and more on searching for the place of possibility. What I find is that often an individual who seemed closed responds to the positive assumption that they can change. One of the powers of subordinate groups is the power to demonize those who are in dominant positions. This demonization may serve to manage the fear and anxiety that usually abounds in situations where dominator culture is the norm, but it is not useful if our goal is to intervene and change structures and individuals.

Since dominator culture promotes and encourages competition, traditional academic settings are not usually locations where colleagues learn to trust one another and to work in mutual partnership. When I forged bonds with white and/or male folks deemed racist and/or sexist by progressive colleagues, I was then viewed by these folks as a "traitor" because I refused to bond on the basis of fixed notions of the enemy. To the extent that I remain ever-mindful of the potential for me to be "the enemy," I am able to view my colleagues who maintain allegiance to dominator culture with compassion. When I demonize them or see them as only and always capable of being enemies, I become part of the problem and not part of the solution. This is especially the case when racism is the issue.

Since racism is about power, it always behooves those of us in subordinate groups to be mindful of our *own* will to power, otherwise we risk asserting power in harmful ways in any situation where we are in the one-up position. Martin Luther King understood this. In his wise sermon "Loving Your Enemies," he contends: "There will be no permanent solution to the race problem until oppressed men develop the capacity to love their enemies . . . For more than three centuries American Negroes have been battered by the iron rod of oppression, frustrated by day and bewildered by night by unbearable injustice, and burdened with the ugly weight of discrimination. Forced to live with these shameful conditions, we are tempted to become bitter and to retaliate with a corresponding hate. But if this happens, the new order we seek will be little more than a duplicate of the old order." The will to dominate knows no color. Every citizen in a dominator culture has been socialized to believe that domination is the foundation of all human relations.

One of the most harmful ideas popularized in the seventies was the assumption that it is not the role of subordinated groups to teach dominate groups how to change. In actuality, to

intervene in dominator culture, to live consciously, we must be
willing to share with anyone knowledge about how to make the
transition from a dominator model to a partnership model. If
we want change, we must be willing to teach. In the civil rights
activism of my youth it was simply accepted that commitment to
anti-racist struggle often meant teaching racists how to unlearn
racism. This notion of not assisting the "oppressor" emerged
from both black power militants working to end racism and
feminist militants working to end sexism. Certainly, the overwhelming global success of civil rights movement to end racism
can be attributed in part to the incredible efforts activists made
to educate citizens of this nation and the world about the hurt
and harm, the exploitation and oppression racism causes.
While people of color need not carry the load when it comes to
educating white folks about racism, our willingness to share
information that challenges and supports change is vital.

When the white male dean interacted with me, his values
were often challenged. He remembers being disturbed as a
teenager as he watched racist acts in the South recalling, "it got
me thinking in ways that I had never thought before." I believe
our interaction, stimulated by the demand for greater diversity
at Oberlin, reawakened this early commitment to anti-racist
action. When interviewed recently and asked if he felt dismay
that no matter the actions he took he was often represented in
a negative light by progressive faculty, he shared that there are
times when he felt dismay. But overall he felt positive about
"staying out of the way and making changes," even if he was
not rewarded for his role. It meant, he says, "that I was doing
something right." Still, I believe it is difficult for any of us to
continue to do what we think is right when we do not receive
affirmation and support.

I came to teach at Oberlin because of a feminist comrade,
Chandra Mohanty; had she not been teaching there I would
not have considered it a place for me. Chandra assured me
that the two of us, two powerful militant brown-skinned femi-

nist scholars, would help transform Women's Studies and the Oberlin campus. She was, and remains, a true comrade in struggle. We did do much positive work at the college, raising awareness around issues of diversity. Yet ultimately neither she nor I was valued rightly. Petty competition, often coming from the very white women colleagues who claimed to be "feminists," made our tasks difficult. Constant power struggles made us both want to leave, and we did. Mohanty went to Hamilton College and I came to City College.

My most recent teaching experience has been as a visiting professor at Southwestern University. After resigning my Distinguished Professorship at City College I truly did not think that I would ever teach again. I came to Texas initially because of the work of Feminist Studies and Philosophy professor Shannon Winnubst. When Shannon first called me, she talked about the way in which my work was widely studied on her campus, revealing both her extensive knowledge of my writing and the ways she had used it and other work by people of color. Openly talking together we discovered a mutual passion for justice. As we made preparations for me to come to and lecture at this predominantly white Methodist liberal arts school, we did the work of building community and solidarity with one another. A white female, a lesbian, Shannon revealed a bold understanding of race, gender, and class. She was the "light" beckoning me to Texas. I mention this to identify the power one individual can have. Singlehandedly, she wooed me to a place where I might never have come except by her courageous example.

After I lectured to a diverse audience of hundreds of students, teachers, and community folk who came to Southwestern's campus to attend my talk, Shannon asked if I would like to come there and teach. I wanted to come and continue our dialogue about justice and building community. Shannon, and other progressive colleagues, talked with the administration and made my appointment possible. They had the support of a progressive white male dean whose field of expertise was education. Contrary to the image of the white male in power who is threatened by any feminist who challenges him, Jim Hunt remembers his first encounter with me was when I came to give the lecture. Committed to creating a more racially diverse campus, he says he was struck by hearing a "complex voice" speaking about issues in a way that went beyond the binary of us/them or oppressor/oppressed. Moved by my discussion of radical openness and the commitment to seeing a world of both/and thinking rather either/or thinking he went to work to bring me to the campus. In the two years I have taught at Southwestern, Jim says that he has come to understand that "people who may be very supportive of difference and diversity in theory are often unable to handle the concrete demands of change." Now he understands better that "learning to live and work in a diverse community" requires a commitment to complex analysis and the letting go of wanting everything to be simple. Segregation simplifies; integration requires that we come to terms with multiple ways of knowing, of interaction.

The process of ending racism in thought and action is always a mutual enterprise. All our power lies in understanding when we should teach and when we should learn. White people who want people of color to do the work for them, who want us to draw the map and then carry them on our back down the road that ends racism are still playing out the servant/served paradigm. But there are also white folks who are simply asking for direction and wanting to talk over the details of the journey. They are doing what any of us do when we work for social change and move from a place of ignorance toward one of greater knowledge. They are our allies in struggle.

Segregation in educational institutions does not move us forward in the struggle to end racism. Teacher and poet Nikki Giovanni believes that a liberal arts education, and particularly one in the humanities, can and should be a location where students and teachers are able to unlearn racism. In *Racism 101* she writes: "It is clear to me that if there is any one crying need in our educational system, it is for the humanities to assert themselves . . . We must reclaim the humanities to remind us that patience is a human virtue; we must integrate racially to show ourselves fear cannot always determine human possibilities."

The segregated schools of my past were the locations where many black folks first were affirmed in our longing to be educated. That affirmation was crucial to our academic development. Yet segregated schools today, particularly in our public school system, function merely as reservations where students are housed, disciplined, and punished, or taught that they cannot achieve academically. In fact students in segregated public schools often feel that they have been "set apart" because no one believes in their capacity to learn. Public schools as well as institutions of higher education must be transformed so that learning is an experience that builds, enhances, and affirms self-esteem. Education can affirm that self-esteem in black students/students of color when educators are anti-racist in word and deed.

White-supremacist thinking can be taught by teachers of any race. Black teachers with internalized racial self-hatred are no better mentors for black students than are white racists. At some predominantly black colleges, white-supremacist thinking still abounds. It articulates itself in many of the same ways racist thinking is perpetuated and maintained in predominantly white educational settings. The dominance of conservative forces in black schools often means that standards of excellence are overdetermined by mainstream thinking about obedience to authority and keeping to the rules. In such settings, educational excellence cannot emerge without struggle. Segregation does not mean that students will be given the best chance to succeed academically.

We can honor the legacy of self-esteem building that originated in segregated schools by studying the strategies teachers in those systems used to educate students fully and well. In the segregated schools of my upbringing, teachers believed in our capacity to excel, to do excellent academic work. This belief set the stage; it was the firm foundation we stood on as we reached for higher learning. When I advise parents about the places to educate black children I urge them to look for settings of racial diversity where teachers are progressive and consciously anti-racist. Oftentimes, black students, like all students, may feel an immediate sense of safety if they are surrounded by people like themselves. This feeling of safety may free them from racial-ized stress and as a consequence they may be more open to learning. But it must be remembered that it is not segregation that creates a context for learning but the absence of racism.

Working to end racism in education is the only meaningful and lasting change that will benefit black students and all stu-dents. Perhaps we will see a day when progressive, non-racist schools, truly educate everyone. They would differ from segre-gated schools in that their premise would be that all students learn and thrive in an anti-racist environment. Significantly, anti-racist educational settings not only protect and nurture the self-esteem of all students, but also prepare students to live in a world that is diverse. The fantasy of white-supremacist exclusion is now pitted against the reality of diversity. People of color who choose to self-segregate as a means of protecting themselves from racial assault cannot avoid facing that diver-sity. To function well in our nation they need to be able to function in diverse settings. They need to know how to to keep their sanity and their intelligence operating in the presence of whiteness and white racist assault. If these skills are not learned then there will be no way for them to meet the challenge of a world that is not yet fully anti-racist but already incredibly diverse. They will not be well equipped to do their part in chal-lenging and changing racism.

In racially integrated educational settings we all have the opportunity to learn in the context of diversity, to be critically conscious of difference without allowing difference to keep us apart. As a black teacher who works most often in predominantly white educational settings I know that teaching students to unlearn racism is an affirmation of their essential goodness, of their humanity. When they are able to drop white supremacy and the quick-fix, phony sense of self-worth it brings them, they are able to discover their real worth as individuals able to face difference without fear. Similarly, the teachers who taught me in all black settings to recognize the limitations of skin color, to seek community with like-minded schools, helped me to understand the value of moving beyond race while always respecting that race matters. In this segregated educational world I was taught to believe that the most vital contribution an educator could make would be to create a context for truth and justice in the classroom. These progressive teachers wanted to see segregation end. They wanted education as the practice of freedom to be the norm in any classroom so that all classrooms would become places where we could learn. It is this revolutionary vision of education we must embrace as we move away from segregation to reclaim the power of anti-racist integration.

Teach 7

How Can We Serve

Commitment to teaching well is a commitment to service. *why does bell think that?* Teachers who do the best work are always willing to serve the needs of their students. In an imperialist white-supremacist capitalist patriarchal culture, service is devalued. Dominator culture pointedly degrades service as a way of maintaining subordination. Those who serve tend to be regarded as unworthy and inferior. No wonder then that there is little positive discussion of the teacher's commitment to serve. Working in public school systems, I meet more teachers who talk openly about service. In the academic world of colleges and universities the notion of service is linked to working on behalf of the institution, not on behalf of students and colleagues. When professors "serve" each other by mutual commitment to education as the practice of freedom, by daring to challenge and teach one another as well as our students, this service is not institutionally rewarded. The absence of reward for service in the interest of building community makes it harder for individual teachers to make a commitment to serve.

Indeed, in colleges and universities excellent teaching is often seen as mere icing on the cake of institutional mainte-nance. Scholarly writing and administrative tasks are deemed the substantive acts. Teaching, and whether or not one does it well, is merely subject to individual choice or whim. Even though every college in our nation uses student evaluations of a teacher's work in the classroom as a factor in job reviews, they are deemed important usually when they are negative and can be used to bolster decisions to dismiss or not promote a pro-fessor. During my undergraduate years I was continually sur-prised by the reality that most of my professors seemed to be uninterested in teaching. They approached the classroom as though teaching was an unwelcome task they needed to com-plete so that they could then go about their real work of writ-ing, thinking, departmental meetings, and so on. Of course, the system of requiring students to take specific courses in order to complete degree requirements has ensured that uncaring professors, whose classes might otherwise be empty, could and can count on full classrooms.

One reason mainstream conservative academics can be so angry about the challenge to racist and sexist biases in educa-tion and the demand for more inclusiveness, is that meeting these demands brought in new and interesting faculty whose courses students wanted to take. There are boring, drunk pro-fessors (usually white and male, but not always) using the same notes they have used for more than twenty years, teaching the usual white male-centered classes. These teachers are still more acceptable to the academy, especially if they have degrees from elite schools, than are women and men who are progressive, who care, who want to make the classroom a com-pelling place for learning. Mass media, particularly newspapers and magazines, have played a major role in misleading the public about the nature of changes in academic environments.

Many Americans, a great many of whom have never been to college, believe that white males are now a minority; that traditional white male-centered classrooms have been eliminated; that black/people of color and feminist white women have taken over. They do not know that despite the powerful interventions of progressive academics to challenge biases, embrace diversity, and support greater inclusion of diverse subject matter, conservative white males still rule in the academy just as they do in our government.

When progressive teachers and their classrooms started to attract a large number of diverse students, a backlash misrepresented these progressive settings as being without standards of excellence, without meaningful material. Even though it was not the case that feminist scholars stopped teaching white males (there may have been a few teachers who felt that there were so many courses focusing on white male perspectives that they could risk not including material by white males), the public was given the impression via mass media that white males were being excluded. Overall, academic women of all races and men of color tended to add new voices to the old voices rather than eliminate the voices of white men altogether. Yet by making the public believe that students were and are being miseducated, reading Alice Walker and not Shakespeare, the conservative white male elites, their colored counterparts, and their non-academic cohorts have been able to exploit the myth of political correctness. Ironically, these conservative academics are often those least interested in teaching.

To many professors of all races, the classroom is viewed as a mini-country governed by their autocratic rule. As a microcosm of dominator culture, the classroom becomes a place where the professor acts out while sharing knowledge in whatever manner he or she chooses. In talking with academic colleagues around the nation, I found that more than eighty percent of the classes many of us attended to acquire doctorate degrees were taught by individuals who lacked basic communication skills. In no other sphere of corporate America would such incompetence be tolerated. Incompetence in teaching can be tolerated because the consumer is a young person who is perceived as having no rights. Subordinated by a hierarchal system that indoctrinates students early on, letting them know that their success depends on their capacity to obey, most students fear questioning anything about the way their classrooms are structured. In our so-called best colleges and universities, teaching is rarely valued.

At its best, teaching is a caring profession. But in our society all caring professions are devalued. No wonder then that professors, especially those at elite institutions, eschew the notion of service as a vital dimension of their work with students in and out of the classroom. In graduate school professors often single out an individual student for praise, even adoration, offering to that student an intensity of engagement denied everyone else. In my graduate experience when this happened the rest of us were made to feel that we were simply not worthy. As students we were socialized to believe that when we entered a classroom and were not regarded with respect by the professor, it was due to some inner lack and not the consequence of unjust hierarchy and dominator culture. The politics of domination as they are played out in the classroom often ensure that students from marginal groups will not do well. Imagine how crazy-making it must be for students coming from an exploited and oppressed group, who make their way through the educational system to attend college by force of a will that resists exclusion, and who then enter a system that privileges exclusion, that valorizes subordination and obedience as a mark of one's capacity to succeed. It makes sense that students faced with this turnabout often do poorly or simply lose interest in education.

As a graduate student who came into the academy from a place of resistance, challenging the sexism of my parents who did not think it important for a female to have a higher degree, challenging the sexism of educators, then confronting racism, I was continually shocked when individual professors, usually white males, would act hatefully toward me. In those naïve years I did not understand the extent to which racist and sexist iconography of the black female body and person had imprinted on the consciousness of many professors the notion that black people in general, and black females in particular, were simply not suited for higher learning. Of course the emotional violence directed at me by professors was not something that could be reported or documented. Contempt, disdain, shaming, like all forms of psychological abuse, are hard to document especially when they are coming from a person in authority, especially one who is skilled in the art of dissimulation. Usually, the only recourse a student has is turning to the peers of their harasser. Fear, especially fear of betrayal, usually silences the student victims of professorial psychological terrorism.

Sometimes professorial harassment of a student is imitated by students. This is often the case when marked differences of race, class, or gender, set a student apart from the group. Group oppression of an individual student deemed unsuitable was depicted in the film *A Beautiful Mind*, where students from privileged class backgrounds assaulted the psyche of a brilliant peer from a working-class background. While the film depicts the forms of psychological terrorism privileged white males use to shame and demean their working-class peer, it then undercuts the message by making it seem that this psychological terrorism was not really meant to hurt, that they meant no harm. Whenever a student is psychologically terrorized by peers or professors there is a tendency to blame the student, to see him or her as misinterpreting reality. No wonder then that students who are victims of psychological assault tend to become passive-aggressive, to remain silent or complain rather than engage in proactive resistance.

Students are so socialized to be docile that they will often critique an uncaring professor's teaching habits and share that

critique with a caring professor. Yet when students have come
to me with horror stories about professors and I suggest they
use boycotts or the power of anonymous letters to express their
opinions they are more often than not unwilling to challenge
the status quo. A brilliant young black female graduate student, who along with several peers bore the brunt of a professor's racist and sexist comments, documented his statements,
then wrote an anonymous letter to the academic dean. The
tenured older white male professor responded by coming to
class and devoting an entire lecture to talk about the "cow-
ardly" student who wrote an anonymous letter. His intent was
to publicly shame the student. The student felt fear and shame
even as she also felt glad to have made a gesture of resistance.
Although her preliminary work toward the doctorate had been
deemed excellent, when it was time for her to go forward in
her studies, no professor, not even the few liberals, wanted to
work with her. Lack of a potential advisor/mentor professor
was the reason given for denying her admission to candidacy
for doctoral work. Even though the student understood the
politics behind this decision she also felt unable to take on the
challenge of continually fighting what she feared would be her
lot if she continued in graduate school. Her experience
reminded me of the many times I was told, and read in my
files, that I did not have the "proper demeanor of a graduate
student," which meant that I dared to challenge my professors
and refused to accept passively their domination.

This gifted young woman dropped out of school, trauma-
tized by her experience of academic injustice. Yet she was truly
excellent in her studies. Often in a dominator context there is
less a concern for whether students are brilliant hard workers
and more a concern with whether they are willing to play the
roles assigned them by professors. On the professorial level this
fixation on demeanor usually surfaces when candidates from
underrepresented groups come to be interviewed by middle-
and upper-class white colleagues who share a common language

and experience. When the candidates are individuals of color coming from working-class backgrounds they may not "fit" with the group norm. The perception that they will not fit may make them lose jobs for which they are eminently qualified. It is a fiction that when faced with excellent students and professors of color predominantly white faculties will affirm and reward brilliance. Time and time again I have witnessed faculties support folks of color that they deem not very smart but hardworkers over individuals who are deep and excellent thinkers and scholars. Sociologists who study race and job performance document the fact that unenlightened white folks have greater suspicion of black folks/people of color who do excellent work than those whose performance is mediocre. They are more comfortable with people of color who act subordinate or are mediocre because this serves as a confirmation bias of their deep-seated belief in the inferiority of non-white groups. *Confirmation bias.* *No black educators*

When I interview black students and scholars who have achieved academic excellence, against the odds I almost always hear stories of the caring professor who functioned as a supportive mentor figure. Psychoanalyst Alice Miller used the term "enlightened witness" to refer to that person who stands with someone being abused and offers them a different model of interaction. Caring teachers are always enlightened witnesses for our students. Since our task is to nurture their academic growth, we are called to serve them.

Commitment to serving the needs of students is not without its pitfalls. It is a counter-hegemonic liberatory practice taking place within a dominator context. Hence students wanting help from progressive educators often come face to face with conflicting desires. They may desire help from an "enlightened witness" while simultaneously desiring to be recognized and rewarded by conventional conservative sources. In states of conflict, students will usually opt to go with the status quo. This experience often leads caring professors to feel cynical about any effort to intervene in the dominator context and engage students with care. Serving students well is an act of critical resistance. It is political. And therefore it will not yield the normal rewards provided when we are simply perpetuating the status quo. The lack of rewards may be less disappointing than rejection by the very students we have served.

A black female student I had mentored throughout her undergraduate years entered graduate school and found that the professors who became her advisors were very critical of my work. She felt torn in her allegiances. When she was writing her master's thesis, and writing way beyond the required number of pages, her primary advisor told her that her work was excellent, even publishable, but that she should work hard to revise, yet again, and not turn in her thesis on time. I shared with the student that I thought this was contradictory advice. If the work was excellent and publishable why not turn it in on time and then revise? Better yet, why not keep some of those extra chapters for dissertation writing? This beloved student, whom I had nurtured for years, accused me of being jealous of her, of believing that she was not capable of finishing work. She was unable to hear my concern that brilliant black female students delay turning work in and never complete their degrees. I did not want her to fall into this category. She never talked with me again.

My disappointment was intense. Yet I could see that this student wanted to become a major player in the existing dominator culture of academe. That desire placed her at odds with maintaining loyalty to me or the values we had shared when she was an undergraduate. I was more concerned that she complete her degree in a reasonable amount of time than that she revise and revise to achieve superlative standing in the eyes of an individual professor. Women of all races and non-white men have been the students that I see most often paralyzed by fears that their work will not be excellent. In such cases I always think it important to be less of a perfectionist and more concerned about completing the work on time.

Every caring teacher knows that our ideas are always in process. Unlike other professions we have the opportunity to return to our written work and make it better. Sadly, students from marginalized groups who have not had a long history in the academy (they are often the first generation in their family to attend college) are often devastated when the work they do is good but not excellent. Perfectionist thinking, reinforced by professors, prevents them from seeing that none of us is excellent all the time. Contrary to much popular misinformation that suggests black students perform inadequately in college because they are indifferent or lazy, much of the inadequacy I see is caused by fear of being less than perfect, of trying to reach standards that are unreachable, thus leading students to despair and self-sabotage.

Teachers who care, who serve their students, are usually at odds with the environments wherein we teach. More often than not, we work in institutions where knowledge has been structured to reinforce dominator culture. Service as a form of political resistance is vital because it is a practice of giving that eschews the notion of reward. The satisfaction is in the act of giving itself, of creating the context where students can learn freely. When as teachers we commit ourselves to service, we are able to resist participation in forms of domination that reinforce autocratic rule. The teacher who serves continually affirms by his or her practice that educating students is really the primary agenda, not self-aggrandizement or assertion of personal power. Conventional pedagogy often creates a context where the student is present in the classroom to serve the will of the professor, meeting his or her needs, whether it be the need for an audience, the need to hear fresh ideas to stimulate work, or the need to assert dominance over subordinated students. This is the tradition of abuse the caring teacher seeks to challenge and change. Commitment to service helps teachers remain accountable to students for ethical content in the classroom. Care and service intervene on managerial notions of classroom conduct.

Commitment to service on the part of teachers bridges the gap between public school education and the teaching that takes place in colleges and universities. In this sense, service restores connection between the various stages of schooling, countering the artificial separation of public school learning and college experience. The teacher who can ask of students, "What do you need in order to learn?" or "how can I serve?" brings to the work of educating a spirit of service that honors the students' will to learn. Committed acts of caring let all students know that the purpose of education is not to dominate, or prepare them to be dominators, but rather to create the conditions for freedom. Caring educators open the mind, allowing students to embrace a world of knowing that is always subject to change and challenge.

Teach 8

Moving beyond Shame

When educators evaluate reasons some students fail while others succeed they rarely talk about the role of shame as a barrier to learning. As conservatives attack policies of affirmative action and other strategies aimed at creating greater diversity in higher education, we hear more and more about the failure of black students who come from similar class backgrounds as their white peers who score highly on standardized tests. We hear about black students who perform below their skills levels. We hear that they are indifferent, lazy, victims who want to work the system so that they get something for nothing. But we do not hear about the politics of shame and shaming.

Throughout the history of civil rights struggle to end racial discrimination, exploitation, and oppression, freedom has often been determined by the degree to which people of color have access to the same privileges as white peers. Embedded in this notion of freedom is the assumption that access is all that is needed to create the conditions for equality. The thinking was: Let black children go to the same schools as white peers and they will have all that is needed to be equal and free. Such thinking denies the role that devaluation and degradation, or all strategies of shaming, play in maintaining racial subordination, especially in the arena of education.

Like all members of subordinated groups who must cope with the negative stereotypes imposed upon them in practically all circumstances where dominators rule, African-Americans have suffered and continue to suffer trauma, much of it the re-enactment of shaming. The self-segregation black folks do in integrated settings, particularly those where white people are the majority group, is a defense mechanism protecting them from being the victims of shaming assaults. In *Facing Shame: Families in Recovery*, Merle Rossum and Marilyn Mason define shame using experiential terms: "Shame is an inner sense of being completely diminished or insufficient as a person. It is the self judging the self. A moment of shame may be humiliation so painful or an indignity so profound that one feels one has been robbed of her or his dignity or exposed as basically inadequate, bad, or worthy of rejection. A pervasive sense of shame is the ongoing premise that one is fundamentally bad, inadequate, defective, unworthy, or not fully valid as a human being." One of the ways racism colonizes the minds and imaginations of black people is through systematic shaming. The primary vehicle for this shaming is the mass media.

Mass media messages equate blackness with being bad, inadequate, unworthy. Little black children comprehend these messages, which are neither subtle are covert. Almost every American owns a television. In most homes the television is on at least seven hours a day. In the essay "Mixed Signals: Race and the Media," Alice Tait and Todd Burroughs offer this fact: "African Americans spend more than 70 hours a week watching television—20 to 35 percent more than whites." Acknowledging the profound power of the media, they contend: "It sets agendas, interprets meaning, confers status, and in its worst case, endorses destructive behavior. Its most powerful impact is on children, who frame definitions and draw conclusions about the world through the messages they receive. Studies conducted in the 1990s show that children across all race associate positive characteristics more with white characters they see on television, and negative characteristics with the minority characters." Few black children are born into a world where they are protected from racist thinking about the nature of blackness. Even if they are raised in predominantly black neighborhoods and attend all-black schools they will be subjected to white-supremacist thinking. Mass media assaults the self-esteem of black children. And it is everywhere.

Looking at the impact of mass media on the self-esteem of black children/children of color is important because they encounter a pedagogy of race and racism long before they enter any classroom settings. Usually schools, unenlightened teachers, and textbooks full of white-supremacist thinking merely reinforce the notion that black children are inferior, unworthy. For example in a classroom where children are taught that Columbus discovered America, as though the continent was previously uninhabited, children are being covertly taught that Native American people and their culture was not worthy or valued. And the sort of diversity in which a teacher adds a section on Native American culture does not intervene on the ingrained perception that native peoples were inferior. Similarly, when black children are taught that the black presence in the "new world" begins with slavery and not with African explorers and traders who came to the "new world" before Columbus or the presence of individual free black Europeans who came in search of treasures before slavery began, the message children receive is that black people are always and only subordinate to white people. Without a counter-narrative (and, thankfully, many black children learn counter-narratives at home so that they can defend themselves against this assaultive mis-information) children of color, black children internalize the belief that they are inferior. If they do not internalize the belief fully they may be consumed by doubt and fear. Wounded or fragile self-esteem leaves the psyche vulnerable—capable of being shamed.

When assaults on self-esteem in public arenas (including school settings) are coupled with traumatic abuse in dysfunctional families, black children coming from these troubled backgrounds must work harder to create healthy self-concepts. Across class, many African-American parents use a discipline-and-punish model that includes shaming. For example, a dark-skinned black child who is told repeatedly at home that they are either bad or that they must try not to be bad internalizes the fear or belief that they are unworthy. According to therapists Gershen Kaufman and Lev Raphael this creates a shaming imprint. In *Coming out of Shame* they provide a lengthy explanation of this shaming process: "Language is another way we reactivate old scenes and reproduce the feelings originally experienced in those scenes. We can synthesize new repetitions of old scenes through language, as when we say the identical phrases to ourselves now that others said to us before. If your mother or father, for instance, said 'You never do anything right' over and over to you as a child, then when you're an adult you're apt to say the identical phrase to yourself, typically in very much the same kind of circumstance. Your parent's phrase became embedded in the original scene, and by repeating that phrase to yourself as an adult you are actually reactivating that scene in the present. When reactivated through either mode—sufficiently similar scenes or language—an old scene intrudes directly in present consciousness, usually with no awareness that it's happening. Then we relive that scene, in the present, with all the force of its original affect." It should not surprise anyone, then, that those black children who have been encouraged to excel academically to prove that they are worthy have ambivalent attitudes toward learning and are vulnerable to shaming.

Even though I was raised in a segregated world where education was valued and I, like all the other children around me, was taught to study hard, to strive for academic excellence, when I left this environment to attend a mainly white college it was unnerving when I had to face the skepticism of white teachers and student peers who found a smart black person an anomaly. Smart black people had always been a given in my life. In white settings the objectification of "smart black people" engendered fear and doubt in me. Just as the constant scrutiny (whether real or merely a fear-based response to being in a racist context) led me to perform poorly for a while. Initially, though I did not consciously understand it, I quickly realized that my self-esteem was being attacked, that this is one of the strategies the dominator used to reinscribe subordination. Unlike individual black students of today, who judge themselves as not worthy of being smart and eschew academic excellence, I was judged by the white people in my environment. Even the liberal white folks who supported and affirmed my presence simultaneously acted as though there was something strange and aberrant about me being black, female, and intellectual. More often than not they, and not the overt racists, were the folks interrogating me about my background. At times I felt as though in their minds I was coming from the "jungle" and they wanted to know "how I escaped."

In the segregated educational environment I came from I had been affirmed as being a good writer. Imagine my sense of bewilderment when in a white setting professors would ask me "Did someone help you write this paper?" Contrary to the notion that black folks are always holding out our racism detectors (like metal detectors), I began college believing fully that my professors believed in my capacity to learn. I was shocked when I was forced to confront the way in which white-supremacist thinking about the nature of race and intelligence surfaced in interactions between professors and myself. Since I had been raised in an environment where resistance to racial

assault and white-supremacist thinking was the norm, I began
to view my professors with a degree of skepticism. Rather than
simply accepting their "judgments" of me and my intelligence,
I sought critical feedback from individuals I could trust.

As long as educators are unwilling to acknowledge the overt
and covert forms of psychological terrorism that are always in
place when unenlightened white people (as well as unenlightened people of color who have internalized white-supremacist
thinking) encounter people of color, especially people of color
who do not conform to negative stereotypes, there can be no
useful understanding of the role shame and shaming plays as
a force preventing marginalized students from performing
with excellence. Recently, lecturing on the issue of self-esteem
at the same institution, I was challenged by a black woman student completing her doctorate, who shared publicly, "I just
don't think that self-esteem is that important." Later in private
conversation she let me know that she had been offered a
teaching job at an Ivy League institution—that her advisors
were suggesting that she would do better at a less prominent
school. I encouraged her first to think about her needs. Then
I asked her to consider if she were a white male doctoral can-
didate with a job offer from an elite school whether he would
be advised not to take the position, to go work at a less distinguished school. My advice to her was to consider choosing the
elite school with a plan to shift to another institution in a few
years. I told her to focus during her years there on being an
excellent teacher and scholar rather than worrying about
whether or not she would be "judged" worthy enough for
tenure in the long run.

When I was offered a job as an assistant professor at Yale
University (my first "real" job) my immediate response was fear
because I was not sure I could "survive" in the Ivy League coming from a working-class background and knowing that I was
not willing to support the dominator culture that was the norm
at that time. Healthy self-esteem allowed me to choose to teach

at Yale and to not go through a tenure process then. Overall it was the most rewarding teaching experience of my entire teaching career. At the time, it was not an institution that was just in its assessment of marginalized individuals when it came to awarding tenure. Understanding this, I left before I was reviewed. I believed that had I allowed unenlightened colleagues to review me they would have endeavored to crush my spirit. Yet none of the racism, sexism, class elitism I encountered at Yale overshadowed the joy in teaching I experienced there, teaching dedicated, committed, brilliant students, many of them students of color and white females. More than ten years have passed since my time at Yale but the students I taught there are still in my life, still allowing me the privilege of teaching them, albeit out of the classroom setting.

Sharing these experiences I hope to call attention to the need for critical vigilance when marginalized students of color (or marginalized individuals of any group, that is, a Jew at a Christian school, a gay person in a predominantly heterosexual and heterosexist environment) enter environments that continue to be shaped by the politics of domination. Without critical vigilance, shaming as a weapon of psychological terrorism can damage fragile self-esteem in ways that are irreparable. Self-esteem is not simply a concern of black folks or individuals from marginalized groups. Many of the professors who teach in colleges and universities have crippling long self-esteem that is covered up by the mantle of power and privilege their positions as educators affords them. Just as white supremacy or male domination serves as a location of privilege that provides pseudo self-esteem, academic hierarchies deem smart people chosen and therefore more worthy of regard than the unintelligent masses. Delegated the "elect," professors who are highly intelligent often feel that it is their role in life to pass judgment on students, to sort out the wheat from the chaff. Usually this sorting-out process includes rituals of shaming. Simply imagine a professor who thinks it important to test students emotionally to see if they have the character to succeed in school or in academic careers standing before a smart black student asking them if they were admitted on the basis of affirmative action or on merit. That question could activate serious feelings of shame. It might, as Kaufman and Raphael contend, evoke memories of childhood scenes when their worth and value as a self was questioned.

Importantly, Kaufman and Raphael identify the "inner voice" of a "scene's conscious residue" that may lead an individual to be self-shaming. For example: a black child told repeatedly that he or she is stupid and not to act stupid before whites may fear being stupid. When faced with a white teacher who treats them like they are stupid these children may activate that internal shaming voice. This can happen with a student who may be exceptionally intelligent but who may discount their worth because the inner voice says that they are really stupid. Kaufman and Raphael state that "the principal effects of shame on the self are hiding, paralysis, and a feeling of being transparent." They contend: "The urge to hide and disappear from view immediately follows shame because we desperately want to reduce the agonizing scrutiny." I would add to this that being the object of intense scrutiny can trigger shame-based re-enactment of painful scenarios. Often black students, students of color, and gay students of all races seek out classes where they are in the majority or social spaces to avoid being "seen" and shamed.

Many black students with excellent academic skill and talent are performing poorly in academic settings because they are shame-based and in settings where shaming is a common practice. In many cases simply the experience of being "judged" activates deep-seated feelings of shame. Messing up, performing poorly eases the anxiety. If the fear is that they will be found wanting, then as soon as they can inappropriately act out so that they are indeed wanting, they can feel better. There are serious taboos against acknowledging shame. Individual black students and colleagues have broken down emotionally as we talk in my office about negative experiences in predominantly white academic settings. They voice shame about feeling shame. One dark-skinned male student confessed that every time he was asked a question in a class where everyone else was white he felt inwardly terrified of failure and he always responded with anger. Even though he could see that this response alienated him from his peers he felt stuck.

With keen insight Kaufman and Raphael identify rage as the most common secondary reaction to shame. They explain: "When the intensity of shame reaches the highest levels, rage is triggered. Rage serves a vital self-protective function: it shields the exposed self. At certain times, rage actively keeps everyone away, covering the self. We refuse further contact because rage has shut us in and others out. But at other times rage in response to shame may make us invite or seek direct contact with whoever has humiliated us—if for no other reason than to strike back . . . That is why if we feel worthless or inadequate . . . we often mask our deeper shame with surface rage." Often individual students of color, and other marginalized students, are consumed by feelings of rage. Their anger blinds them, preventing them from taking needed steps to restore their integrity of being and personal agency.

Until the power of shaming is taken seriously as a threat to the well-being of all students, particularly individuals from marginalized and/or subordinated groups, no amount of support staff, positive programming, or material resources will lead to academic excellence. Many white male professors entered college as students fully aware that they might be subjected to rituals of shaming to prove their worth, their right to be one of the chosen. As a consequence they may endure these rituals without feeling threatened or destroyed. Not so for vulnerable students from marginalized groups who may enter college (often as the first member of their family to attend) with no awareness that ritualized shaming may take place. Rituals of shaming may create in them a true crisis of spirit where they doubt both their self-worth and their reason for being in college. Often students experiencing such crises feel as though they are losing their minds. They recover themselves only as they work to come out of shame. They recover themselves only when there are progressive educators who give them space to feel their shame, express those feelings, and do the work of healing.

Academics who use shaming to crush the spirit of students who challenge and interrogate all they are learning, the environments in which they come to learn, and the teachers whose classrooms they enter, are engaged in forms of emotional violence. They are abusive. Though rarely explicitly stated, their violence is often committed in the name of maintaining imperialist white-supremacist patriarchal hegemony in the academic world. Students should not and cannot bear the sole responsibility for challenging these individuals. Professors must dare to critically intervene not just on behalf of an individual student, but also on behalf of our teaching profession. When a black female student confessed to two white female professors, both feminist scholars, that she was repeatedly shamed by a white male professor, they investigated. They intervened. Their intervention was the act of critical resistance that affirmed the student's right to be respected, to be educated, her right to well-being at a predominantly white college; it affirmed her self-esteem.

As long as educational institutions continue to serve as settings where the politics of domination in any form are perpetuated and maintained, teachers will need to confront the issue of shame. Conveying genuine respect for colleagues and students (especially those deemed other or different) we can affirm everyone's right to self-determination. Kaufman and Raphael remind us that "all human beings stand equal in the sudden exposure wrought by shame." They state: "Shame shadows each of us, and everyone encounters the alienating effect in some form, at some time. Entering that experience long enough to endure it, deliberately, and consciously in order to transform it, is a challenge which knows no bound. Yet only by facing that challenge can we ever hope to re-create who we are." While writing specifically about the experiences of gay people coming out of shame, Kaufman and Raphael offer insights that pertain to any member of a marginalized, exploited, or oppressed group, or any individual experiencing the detrimental affects of traumatic shaming.

When education as the practice of freedom is affirmed in schools and colleges we can move beyond shame to a place of recognition that is humanizing. Shame dehumanizes. There can be no better place than the classroom, that setting where we invite students to open their minds and think beyond all boundaries to challenge, confront, and change the hidden trauma of shame. We do this by enacting a politics of affirmation where difference is accorded respect and all voices deemed worthy. As teachers we can make the classroom a place where we help students come out of shame. We can allow them to experience their vulnerability among a community of learners who will dare to hold them up should they falter or fail when triggered by past scenarios of shame—a community that will constantly give recognition and respect.

Teach 9

Keepers of Hope

Teaching in Communities

When I first published *Teaching to Transgress: Education as the Practice of Freedom* I included a dialogue with Ron Scapp. We have the pleasure of being both colleagues and true friends. In his new book *Teaching Values: Critical Perspective on Education, Politics, and Culture* Ron states; ". . . there is a real need (an ethical imperative) to disrupt and challenge the simple acts of privilege, and that one of the ways to begin this process is by listening to and acknowledging those for whom such acts are not simple. So clearly, for a white, heterosexual, male, tenured professor of relative financial security this means reading, listening to, and speaking with, among others, people of color." We still live in a culture where few white people include black people/people of color in their intimate kinship structures of love and friendship on terms that are fully and completely anti-racist. We still need to hear about how inclusion of diversity changes the nature of intimacy, of how we see the world. When

I walk out into the world with Ron, clearly indicating closeness by our body language and our speech, it changes how I am seen, how he is seen. This is yet another way race matters in a white-supremacist patriarchal context. It is still important for us to document these border crossings, the process by which we make community. This dialogue extends the first. It was spontaneous—neither of us had questions beforehand or altered what we said after the fact. It is shared as a way to bear witness to real community, real love, and what we do to keep it real.

bell hooks: Ten years have passed since we first dialogued together about the intersections of race, class, gender and their impact on our teaching and learning communities, on our attempts to bond as colleagues, as friends. Since that time you have become much more engaged with setting educational policy and dialoguing with policy makers. What are some of the key issues you face talking to people from a non-biased perspective who are still stuck—who are still supporting race, sex, class hierarchies?

Ron Scapp: One ongoing issue is the effort to build trust. Many people who occupy positions that afford them the opportunity to set educational policy are often distrustful from the start when encountering anyone who claims to offer anti-racist strategies, particularly new insights.

bh: Say more about why trust is important.

RS: Trust is such a fundamental issue because these people are so invested in all that they have put into operation already. They may feel the need to protect the status quo. Any challenge, but especially one that hints at racism on their part, makes them particularly wary because of what it suggests about them. My goal is to let them know that we share a common concern for making education better—for creating optimal conditions for all students to learn and teachers to do their best work; that's the common goal we can share and the foundation for us to trust one another.

bh: This fear of being found personally wanting in some way is often one of the greatest barriers to promoting critical consciousness, especially about racist and sexist domination. Since the practice of critical thinking requires that we all engage in some degree of critical evaluation of self and other, it helps if we can engage individuals in ways that promote self-motivated interrogation rather reactive response to outer challenge.

RS: Policy makers often hear challenges as personal attacks and don't see the person making the challenge as a team player who wants to better the circumstances of teachers and students.

bh: What are some of the strategies you use to intervene on this fear and create a sense of shared community and concerns?

RS: One effort I make when addressing a smaller group of policy makers is to share stories as a gesture of intimacy, making personal contact, specifically acknowledging moments in my teaching and administrative work where I had to engage in critical vigilance and see the residual impact of racism influencing my decision-making process.

bh: In the years since we first began talking together I have learned that when people feel directly threatened (as in "You are labeling me a racist or sexist") they simply shut down or become crazily defensive. Like you, I rely on the sharing of personal narratives to remind folks that we are all struggling to raise our consciousness and figure out the best action to take. Even so, we are not all committed to education as the practice of freedom. I'm sure you encounter many folks who don't see freedom as connected in any way to education.

RS: While these folks can short-circuit genuine dialogue what does often happen is that they become less significant for their peers when more progressive voices speak clearly from the location of lived experience without a tone of moral or political superiority. This allows folks who usually hesitate before speaking or remain silent to begin to address their own prejudice or habitual reactions. They engage in critical dialogue. An example of this is the statement that "racism is over, they've had every opportunity given to them and still they are complaining." People say, "Why should we spend more money on new resources for poor urban students when so much money has been sunk in, leveling the playing field, and yet the results do not reflect significant change?" I respond by calling attention to the many instances where students from middle- and upper-class communities receive additional resources directly from their own families (tutoring for academic skills, coaching for sports) in addition to receiving material resources (i.e., up-to-date computer programs and hardware) that give them a clear academic advantage. When I point out that students from privileged backgrounds are still predominantly white, it highlights the fact that race and class continue to play a major role in academic preparedness.

bh: Conservatives, though, like to point to the fact that black students from privileged backgrounds do more poorly on standardized tests than poor white students. To them this proves that class is not a factor. In actuality they are assuming that class is solely about money and not about shared cultural experiences, common language. Certainly the language deployed in these tests is a direct reflection of racialized codes as much as class codes. A black middle-calss student may have the same material resources as a white middle-class student but operate within radically different cultural codes.

RS: One aspect of my task as a progressive educator is to constantly delineate these differences and help folks understand that these things affect how and why students learn or not.

bh: What has most changed about your thinking in the last ten years as you have attempted to create greater awareness of the need for non-biased ways of knowing?

RS: The single most important realization has been the need to establish a genuine sense of community based on trust—in my teaching practice and in my administrative work—and not just expertise and knowledge. It's a simple observation, but this does not diminish its vitality and power. Many professors and schoolteachers working with diverse populations are challenged to recognize the importance of genuine commitment to the well-being and success of all students and not simply those deemed worthy because they come from privileged backgrounds. Teachers and professors cannot assume that because they hold valuable information that students need to know this will automatically lead to a feeling of community.

bh: Creating trust usually means finding out what it is we have in common as well as what separates us and makes us different. Lots of people fear encountering difference because they think that honestly naming it will lead to conflict. The truth is our denial of the reality of difference has created ongoing conflict for everyone. We become more sane as we face reality and drop sentimental notions like "We are all just human, just the same," and learn both to engage our differences, celebrating them when we can, and also rigorously confronting tensions as they arise. And it will always be vital, necessary for us to know that we are all more than our differences, that it is not just what we organically share that can connect us but what we come to have in common because we have done the work of creating community, the unity within diversity, that requires solidarity within a structure of values, beliefs, yearnings that are always beyond the body, yearnings that have to do with universal spirit.

RS: This is especially important for those of us who are committed to education as a way to support genuine democratic process and social justice. Enabling students to think critically on their own allows them to resist injustice, to come together in solidarity, to realize the promise of democracy.

bh: In your recently published book *Teaching Values* you urge progressive educators to refuse to surrender the discourse of values to the Right and to make ourselves heard, naming the values that we embrace and that are essential to democratic process, to education as the practice of freedom.

RS: Values like generosity of spirit, courage, the willingness to reconsider long-standing beliefs.

bh: Which is what I call radical openness. Even though I disagreed with many of the arguments in the *Closing of the American Mind,* I loved the title because it strategically evoked the value of openness even as the book did not support open-minded thinking. The will to keep an open mind is the safeguard against any form of doctrinaire thinking, whether coming from the Right or Left.

RS: The Right's insistence that progressive education leads to cultural and moral relativism prevented genuine dialogue about the values which underlie democracy.

bh: One of the most powerful uses of mass media has been the false representation of progressive professors as the culprits shutting down debate on university campuses and in school districts, and not the forces of the Right closing the door to all ways of thinking that offer an alternative to dominator culture. And, yes, we know that there are individuals who critique dominator culture who are rigid in their thinking, but they are not more rigid than their conservative counterparts. Nor do they constitute a greater threat. Indeed, a student encountering a progressive educator who is doctrinaire is far more likely to be guided away from political correctness or any close-minded thinking by the different teaching voices they will learn about along the way. Whereas the Right, who are rigid, rarely include in their course outline a variety of material from a broad spectrum of academic perspectives and political persuasions.

RS: This is why progressive educators, democratic educators, must be consistently vigilant about voicing hope and promise as well as opposition to those dominating forces that close off free speech and diminish the power of dialogue.

bh: Our dialogues together stimulate us. They lead us back to the drawing board and help us strengthen ideas. We have continued to support each other as friends, as colleagues, crossing the boundaries of race, gender, and status. In these past ten years I have resigned a tenured position while you have solidified your place in the academy. As our locations change, our dialogue also changes. I worry that you as an administrator will be sucked more and more into a conventional hierarchy that will change your language and cause you to speak from the very locations of privilege, race, and gender that you have so consistently critiqued.

RS: That's a real and genuine consideration. But that's part of the fun of having close comrades who challenge you and keep you honest about your position.

bh: You and I have together strengthened the bonds of personal closeness and professional solidarity by always maintaining a space where we listen to one another when the other is raising critical questions, when we interrogate each other. Certainly on matters of race, I often bring to you the perspective of someone who sees the world differently because of the different locations I am placed in that you, as a white male, will not be given access to.

RS: Again, I want to state that this is why the building of trust through a process of concrete action, along with cultivating the values of courage and civility, combined with commitment to community, is needed if we are to find unity within diversity. These are all essential qualities that must be cultivated when we seek to build friendship, partnership—inside the academy, in public schools (one of the last bastions of state-supported democracy), and in every setting where values are challenged and embraced.

bh: Can you talk about what you think and how you feel when I challenge you? Like the time you were talking to me in a manner that I felt evoked white male superiority and I told you "Ron, you are being too directive." How does it feel when I criticize you? Most of the time you see yourself as the good guy, the guy who is out there busting his butt to work for justice in everyday life and in the classroom. We both know that, but you can always assume a position that reinscribes white male privilege.

RS: Like the many people I challenge, I too feel the emotion, the embarrassment, and the anger when I feel accused of being a dominator, however gently that accusation is made, or how accurately. But then I have cultivated the ability to pause and critically consider my actions, to reflect. This is the critical practice that makes solidarity possible, not that we never make mistakes or ever rid ourselves of the fear of being racists or dominators, or of simply hurting others by our ignorance.

bh: One of the most challenging moments of our intellectual intimacy and our friendship occurred when I was being filmed by my beloved friend and comrade Marlon Riggs for the film *Black Is, Black Ain't.* I had invited you to come to the studio without thinking about race. Once true intimacy is formed across difference it is not that we forget our differences, but they in no way insert themselves as inequalities or unjust power levers that separate us so that we stop thinking about the significance of race or gender, at least when we are together. While I do not forget that you are a good-looking white man (this is a looks-oriented culture, from grade school on we know how much looks determine whether individuals will be treated justly, respectfully) this never means that you assert yourself as a dominator or that I accept your using white male privilege.

RS: That was a very emotional day. We both walked in and felt the intensity of his conflicting moods. Even though I was welcomed, it was clear that I was being checked out.

bh: As part of your respect for the politics of race you had already stated that if your presence was in any way "disruptive" you would leave. Still, I realized that I needed to check it out with Marlon before I arrived at the studio with a straight white male. He was cool about it. Yet when we arrived it was clear that everyone else was black, that I was the only female and you the only white person, that gay and bi-sexual folks were in the majority. My being went on red alert. I knew this might be (as it was) my last time working with Marlon. He was sick and in the process of slowly dying, past that point where you know there is a chance of a miracle. The miracle was that he was so sick and yet working hard, so alive, yet already in the arms of death. This was a profoundly intimate moment.

RS: Being in that setting, I knew I had to be respectful of the whole mood. Most of the time white men allow themselves to deny awareness, to keep from sensing moods and being empathic. Feeling the mood, being open comes from a practice of respect, a willingness to acknowledge up front that you may not and will not be automatically accepted everywhere you go. The practice of "pausing" is a practice of respect. It allows you to acknowledge and access other's peoples feelings without violating that space with your insistence that you have a right to be there, or anywhere you want to be. By pausing, by demonstrating deference to those who may reject you, to give them the opportunity to be in doubt and to possibly reject you is one way to repudiate white male privilege, and one way to allow others to be in the position of the chooser, the authority.

bh: That's such an important life lesson because often it is those white folks who want to hang in the space of blackness who are most freaked out if they are not allowed immediate, uninterrogated access. They are often the folks who are enraged if their desire to hang is denied, deferred, or if it simply is not an appropriate moment for them to be present.

RS: This is why it's important when we are challenging racism or any unjust hierarchy to accept moments of awkwardness, embarrassment, and maybe even rejection. To acknowledge that possibility without refusal, to accept the judgments of those deemed other. We are still wanting as white folks to be at the center even if we are in the minority.

bh: We learned that day how much our emotional awareness can serve as a force to bind us together in community and enable us to transcend difference. That day we were all bound together in a heavenly solidarity. It was such a moving experience. Race, gender, sexual labels all those human constructs gave way to the emotional experience of creating art in the face of impending loss. You were present fully in the moment. Nothing about your whiteness separated you from us. The presence of death can do that. It can make us put everything in proper perspective.

RS: That feeling of community that reaches beyond boundaries only happened because of the incredible generosity of everyone present. Trust was established at the onset when I showed by my behavior that I was not there to take over and was fully prepared to stay and be silent, to do whatever task assigned to me, or to leave. Instead, this experience of your sharing space, of heterosexuals being guided by the genius and creativity of gay black men, brought us closer together. Our friendship was shared and witnessed as we showed, by our interaction, that we can be together, critique whiteness, dismantle structures of privilege and let love that is rooted in partnership be the tie that binds us.

bh: Our friendship, which has been fundamentally rooted in anti-racist activism, in sharing our vulnerabilities and our strengths always gives me hope. Just when I feel that the vast majority of white men are hopeless because of their stubborn refusal to work for justice and change, you share some story about your work, about the way you have conducted yourself in the world, that reminds me change is possible, that the struggle is ongoing.

RS: Your presence in my life these many years has provided support, direction, and love. If I could share what I have learned from my experience of bonding with an incredibly powerful intelligent feminist black woman, it would be that honest, just, and passionate engagement with difference, otherness, gives me the opportunity to live justly with love. Difference enhances life. This is not to be confused with shallow notions of inclusiveness or experiencing diversity where one stands in the space of privilege, taking in and from those who are other. But rather where one is fundamentally moved—transformed utterly. The end result of this transformation is mutuality, partnership, and community.

bh: Tragically, people have been told, especially since the tragic events of September 11, the lie that encountering difference will diminish their spirits rather than afford them the opportunity to nurture spiritual and intellectual growth in new and varied ways. This dialogue is yet another occasion for us to bear witness, to be examples of solidarity between a white male and a black female that is abiding and life sustaining. Just as our relationship provides us with needed intimacy and love, we bear witness publicly to engender hope, to let readers know that genuine connection and community is possible.

Teach 10

Progressive Learning

A Family Value

Just as the family is often a training ground for life in community, it is the place where we are first given a sense of the meaning and power of education. In Scott Sanders' memoir *Hunting for Hope* he reminds us: "Family is the first community that most of us know. When families fall apart, as they are doing now at an unprecedented rate, those who suffer through the breakup often lose faith not only in marriage but in every human bond. If compassion won't reach across the dinner table, how can it reach across the globe . . . Many of the young people who come to me wondering how to find hope are wary of committing themselves to anyone because they've already been wounded in battles at home. . . . I remain hopeful about community, because my own experience of family, in spite of strains, has been filled with grace." The crisis in families that Sanders describes has created an educational crisis. The dysfunctional, more often than not patriarchal family, is often a rule-bound autocratic system where the will to learn is crushed early in the spirit of children and adult females Irrespective of class or educational level, families that support children and adults who are seeking to educate themselves provide a positive foundation.

Even though my mother had not finished high school (she did her work to receive a diploma late in life), when we were growing up, she instilled in all her children the desire to learn. In this she was supported by our dad who we saw and see consistently reading, consistently informing himself about the events of the world. Dad was and is a critical thinker. As a working-class man influenced by the cultural milieu of the forties, guided by the works of Paul Robeson, James Baldwin, and Roy Campanella, black male writers whose books were in his bookcase, he embodied for us the importance of learning to read and think, of critical literacy. Now elderly, Veodis and Rosa Bell Watkins continue to support all their children in their efforts to be educated. They supported seven children attending colleges. They are proud of the teachers in their family. And yet it has not been an easy process for them to be the parents of a "famous" intellectual who often uses their life stories as part of her teaching lessons. They are not always happy with what I say, and they do not always positively affirm my right to say it. However they consistently support me. Their "fidelity" and loyalty to me, along with the support of my siblings—my sisters and brother—has been an important source of sustenance for me when I dare to create and present ideas to a world that is not yet fully open to those ideas.

Concerned about the ethics of sharing material from their lives, using their stories in my work, more often than not I talk with family first, to see if my writing about them is acceptable. Of course, there are times when they agree and yet still feel upset, disturbed, and sometimes downright angry when they read my work and what I say about them. Years ago I wrote this letter to Veodis and Rosa Bell Watkins:

"I am writing you both to say that I am sorry that my public sharing of experiences that have deeply affected me hurts you. It is not my intention or desire to cause you pain. And if my actions are hurting, please be forgiving. All my life I have worked to be an open, honest person who has nothing to hide, who does not feel shame about anything that has happened in my life and while I have chosen to talk about painful memories in my work, I also speak about joyful memories. There is nothing about the pain of the past that I have not forgiven, but forgiveness does not mean that one forgets. It is my deep belief that in talking about the past, in understanding the things that have happened to us we can heal and go forward. Some people believe that it is best to put the past behind you, to never speak about the events that have happened which have hurt or wounded us, and this is their way of coping—but coping is not healing. By confronting the past without shame we are free of its hold on us.

When I talk with family, friends, or anyone else about past events it is not to blame or to suggest that everything was "bad" or to imply that you, my parents, were these horrible people. Sincerely, I believe you two, mom and dad, did the best job of raising us that you could do given your circumstances—everything that happened to you in your families of origin, much of which has been unresolved trauma. I appreciate all the care that you both give to me; that appreciation can and does co-exist with critical awareness of things that were done that were not positive, loving, or nurturing of my emotional and spiritual growth.

As a writer who has chosen to do autobiographical writing, to share stories in critical essays, I realize that I share information publicly that you would not share. My hope is that you will respect my right to tell my story as I see it even though you do not always agree with what is being told or the decision to speak openly about family matters publicly.

Over the years I feel especially proud of the way in which we have talked together. I am proud of my closeness with you, Dad, since we were estranged for so long. While I know Dad does not always agree with my perspective I trust that he will continue to respect my choices as I respect his need to be silent—to refuse memory. Dad, I love you very much. My talking about the pain of the past does not mean that I am angry at you or unforgiving. Indeed, I am proud of the way you have grown and become a caring and loving man over the years and I admire you for this; we all do. In your actions you have certainly made amends for the past. And I believe you understand the reasons why I, a writer, a critical thinker, an intellectual, speak of things that are difficult. Maybe if you share this understanding with mom, she will not be so hurt and angry. You both taught us that "we are never too old to learn."

Sharing painful memories does not negate positive memories. If there had not been many wonderful aspects of my childhood I would not seek to strengthen our closeness, to talk with you about my being, my work. It's the presence of so much "good" that keeps us together as a family. To stay together, to cherish our closeness, then, we have to be open and honest—sharing both our joy and our pain."

Always seeking to share knowledge with family, with my parents and siblings, I encounter difficulties. It is oftentimes a struggle, especially confronting the sexism of my dad and my brother. I have never wanted to be an educator who offers knowledge in the classroom that I do not seek to share in family settings, thereby creating a disjuncture between what I do as work and how I live in intimate settings. The closed-minded thinking I challenge in classrooms must often be challenged in our family, from internalized racial self-hatred, homophobia, to the Christian fundamentalism that sees all other religious practices as Satanism. Just as I openly challenge family members I must be open to their critiques of me and my ideas. This mutual willingness to listen, to argue, to disagree, and to make peace is the positive outcome of our collective commitment as a family to learning. This is education as the practice of freedom.

Modest and humble, Rosa Bell and Veodis, Mom and Dad, both stated that my success is a reflection of my ability and not their input. This is simply not so. Their support of education made a powerful impression on me. My mother, Rosa Bell, was not raised in a family where education mattered (her mother could not read or write). Mama says: "I urged all of you to study because I wanted you to have the opportunity I did not have." An avid reader as a child, Mama's educational dreams, her dreams of becoming a writer were not fulfilled. She has not yet decided to take college classes even though all of us (her children) encourage her to do so. She says she is not at all surprised that I am an outspoken supporter of free speech and a well-known intellectual because "you were always interested in performing; you loved reading and writing." Dad acknowledges that he is surprised that I have become so well known because "even though you were a smart girl, you were always a bit 'touched' [crazy] and just a bit shy."

Everyone in our family shares books we like to read with one another. Although everyone complains about watching films with me, they want to hear what I think. Our brother Kenneth decided that we should all watch *Titantic* together because it was a film that moved him. It was a film I would never have chosen. We watched it and then we had a lively critical debate about it. When I work with working-class families who are concerned that their children are not reading or writing, I emphasize the importance of shared family time reading and engaging in discussion, even if that time is only ten minutes. I share the importance of engaging in critical discussion of what we see on television and in movies.

Sarah and Theresa, my two oldest sisters, are both women who speak their minds. Sarah is a schoolteacher and Theresa works at a mental hospital. Theresa is the sibling who always affirms me and never feels threatened by what I write about. While growing up she was also punished for being outspoken, so she understands the need to protect free speech, dissident voices. Sarah buys more bell hooks books than any other family member even though I would happily send them to her. She has been angry in the past about the work, mostly because she sees the way it causes Mama pain. As the eldest, she has always been closer to Mama and more of a protector.

Even though I engage in passionate dialogue with all my family members, my five sisters Sarah, Theresa, Valeria, Gwenda, Angela, and our brother Kenneth, I share my work most with my sisters Gwenda and Valeria because the work they do has shared points of convergence with mine. Valeria is a clinical psychologist. We live together in a duplex. Each of us has our own place and the books travel up and down the stairs. Gwenda teaches middle school in Flint, Michigan; she has also worked as an acting principal. Gwenda often invites me into her classroom to dialogue her students and the entire school. She also joins me at various conferences and talks. Telling me "I feel a little in awe—just in awe of your ability to stand up before audiences and speak, to speak your mind, telling it like it is, without fear." Of all my siblings, Gwenda has been the most understanding about my using autobiography in my work, even when our interpretations differ. She feels that I have taught her a lot about self-esteem, that "if you are truly giving of yourself much will be returned to you." Watching me she says she has learned "education is power." Intially she did not finish her bachelor's degree because she married and became a mother and a homemaker. As she acquired feminist consciousness, she was motivated to return to school. She confesses that she visited me in California and I interrogated her about her life, asking her if she was fulfilled. This made her think. My support, both emotional and financial, helped bolster her zeal to return and finish her undergraduate degree, then begin a master's program, which she has now completed.

Gwenda feels that the most important reward of study and learning, of going back to school has been self-actualization, independence, greater self-esteem. Like our mother, Gwenda

is married to a patriarchal man who has not been wholeheartedly supportive of her educational efforts or her professional
career. She says: "Even though the change in my life has been
for the better it has not made it less difficult." Gwenda would
not have called herself a feminist years ago but "today—yes."
Her ideas changed because she "learned that it was acceptable
to be a feminist thinker." From reading bell hooks and other
feminist writers she acquired "a real understanding of feminism." Before that she had "the old stereotypes in my mind." I
ask her why she is not listening to me when I encourage her to
get a Ph.D. She responds: "I'm listening." But she feels that she
has to make this move "when the time is right for me. This
does not mean when things are perfect because things are not
going to be perfect but there is a right time." When that time
comes I will be there to support and affirm all her efforts.

When Valeria chose to leave her career as a therapist and
hospital administrator to return to school, she really made the
connection between all that she had read in my writing about
education and her graduate school experience. During her
graduate school years we had more dialogues about the intersection of racism and sexism than at any other time in our
lives. An out lesbian, she is committed to working to end
homophobia, to making sexual freedom for everyone an everyday reality; this is work we share.

Our brother Kenneth has had the greatest difficulty with
my writing about his experiences. Kenneth feels more comfortable with me talking about his childhood than about problems he has faced in his adult life. He wants to move past the
stigma of being associated with problems related to addiction
and be seen as he is in his life now. Kenneth feels he has
learned much from my insights, especially reading about the
combination of reason and intuition that he has seen me using.
All his sisters have helped him learn more about the nature of
sexism, but he says: "I'm still a sexist." He relates his clinging
to patriarchy to our father's investment in patriarchy. Kenneth

says that he knows women are his equals, but that he often
feels he has to have the last word. Like all of us he feels that
"education is the ticket. Without it you just stay in the same
place." Kenneth feels education is important for emotional
and spiritual growth even if it does not lead to greater social
mobility.

Our youngest sister Angela has really struggled the most to
achieve her goals against the odds. She was once in a difficult
marriage where there was domestic violence. Leaving that relationship challenged all her values. I can remember her initial
anger at my sending her feminist books about domestic violence. Now she says: "I don't have a problem with being written about; however, there are personal things I may not want
to share with everyone. "Angela's feels that she has learned
from me "that it is fine to be different—to go after your dream
no matter what anyone else thinks of you." When asked about
feminism she states: "I feel that I am a feminist in a lot of ways.
I have learned about feminism from books and from other critically thinking females." I always tell her how smart she is and
that she should finish college and go on to graduate school.
She says: "I am reluctant because I'm not motivated to go back
to school. It's about commitment." Like all of us, she is constantly reading.

Oftentimes when I am lecturing about my past, I am asked
what allowed me to move beyond the boundaries set by race,
religion, gender, and class. I always state that critical thinking
helped me move my life in the direction that I wanted it to go.
Although obedience was primary in our patriarchal household, in its subcultures (the world we created when Dad was at
work or not around) we were encouraged to know our own
minds and to speak from our hearts. Mama remembers: "You
were always committed to speaking the truth even when you
were little." Of all my family members she has been the most
hurt by my discussions of our family life. She likes to insist that:
"I tell lies." I understand her pain because she is the person in

our family who has worked the hardest to keep us all together, to care for us, to support us as we endeavored to educate ourselves. When I asked Mama how she copes with the hurt she feels, the sense that she has been betrayed by me, she responds by saying: "I pray. I ask that the pain will be taken away." Of course I hope that greater awareness, more education for critical consciousness will take place in Mom's life and that this awareness will not only ease the pain but create a new space of freedom.

Mr. V. (a nickname I have for Dad) is impressed he says "by the way you use your mind." Although he does not agree with much that I write about him he stands by my right to "write what I feel." He has worked to change mama's thinking. Dad says he tells her: "You were putting down what you wanted to write. She's writing the way she sees things. Anybody that writes, writes the way they see it, they write how they feel about it. You got to respect that and not try to change it." Dad has traveled abroad and read much non-fiction writing. He fought in the all-black infantry during World War II. All this has helped him have a global perspective. Like the men of his generation he is a "race man." More than our mother he brought a critique of whiteness and white power into our home.

His own reading began in childhood. The white people his single mother worked for gave him used books. When I asked how he learned about the work of Paul Robeson, James Baldwin, and many other black writers he remembers that he learned a lot from reading *Life* magazine, which he says "was a white magazine but they carried a lot of articles about black folks." Dad was the book buyer in the family. And when Mama wanted to buy us books he made the final decision. The last book I gave him was a book on black male style, and even though his grandson wanted him to give it away, dad was adamant that this was a book he wanted to read.

Interviewing my family, I had hoped that they would speak more about the difficulties; I know it has not been easy for them. We are coming from different locations in our lives—some of us are poor or working-class, others are economically well-off; some of us finished high school and either did not go to college or went late in life; some of us are fundamentalist Christians, as we were raised to be, and some of us are into Buddhism. We are different. Coping with so much difference in my own family has helped me as an intellectual and a critical thinker. Hence my tremendous gratitude to my family for always communicating and doing the work with me of creating community.

Teach 11

Heart to Heart

Teaching with Love

To speak of love in relation to teaching is already to engage a dialogue that is taboo. When we speak of love and teaching, the connections that matter most are the relationship between teacher and subject taught, and the teacher-student relationship. When as professors we care deeply about our subject matter, when we profess to love what we teach and the process of teaching, that declaration of emotional connection tends to be viewed favorably by administrators and colleagues. When we talk about loving our students, these same voices usually talk about exercising caution. They warn us about the dangers of getting "too" close. Emotional connections tend to be suspect in a world where the mind is valued above all else, where the idea that one should be and can be objective is paramount. Both during my student years and throughout my career as a teacher I have been criticized for having too much passion, for being "too" emotional.

I have been told again and again that emotional feelings impede one's capacity to be objective. Discussing objectivity in *To Know as We Are Known,* Parker Palmer states: "The root meaning of 'objective' is 'to put against, to oppose.' This is the danger of objectivism: it is a way of knowing that places us in an adversarial relation to the world . . . Indeed objectivism has put us in an adversarial relation to one another." Throughout my student years I noticed that the professors who valued objectivism highly were often individuals who lacked basic communication skills. Often pathologically narcissistic, they simply could not connect. At times they experienced as a threat any efforts students made to emotionally connect with them. It was their inability to connect that helped me interrogate their overevaluation of objectivity. They stood at a distance from us (students) and the world, and yet I could see no evidence that this distance made them see everything more clearly, or enabled them to be just or fair. Certainly, the argument in favor of objectivity was that it freed us from attachments to particular individuals or perspectives.

Objectivity was made synonymous with an "unbiased standpoint." The professors who prided themselves on their capacity to be objective were most often those who were directly affirmed in their caste, class, or status position. Parker contends: "The oppression of cultural minorities by a white, middle-class, male version of 'truth' comes in part from the domineering mentality of objectivism. Once the objectivist has 'the facts,' no listening is required, no other points of view are needed. The facts, after all, are the facts. All that remains is to bring others into conformity with objective 'truth.'" It is this will to bring others into conformity that merges with the will to dominate and control, what Parker calls 'the domineering mentality of objectivism.' Where there is domination there is no place for love.

Embedded in the notion of objectivity is the assumption that the more we stand at a distance from something the more we look at it with a neutral view. This is not always the case. Still it is a way of thinking about knowledge that continues to hold sway over the minds of professors who fear getting too close to students and to one another. Explaining the dialectics of objectivism Parker Parker writes; "the ideal of objectivism is the knower as 'blank state,' receiving the unadulterated imprint of what facts are floating around. The aim of objectivism is to eliminate all elements of subjectivity, all biases and preconceptions, so that our knowledge can become purely empirical." While objectivism can work well in hard sciences and more fact-oriented subjects, it cannot serve as a useful basis for teaching and learning in humanities classrooms. In these classrooms much of what students seek to know requires engagement not just with the material but with the individual creators whose work we study.

At times objectivism in academic settings is a smokescreen, masking disassociation. In *Lost in the Mirror*, psychotherapist Richard Moskovitz describes dissociation as "a defense mechanism in which experiences are sorted into compartments that are disconnected from one another." Teachers who fear getting close to students may objectify them to maintain the valued objectivity. They may choose to think of students as empty vessels into which they are pouring knowledge, vessels without opinions, thoughts, personal problems, and so forth. Denying the emotional presence and wholeness of students may help professors who are unable to connect focus more on the task of sharing information, facts, data, their interpretations, with no regard for listening to and hearing from students. It makes the classroom a setting where optimal learning cannot and will not occur.

When teachers and students evaluate our learning experiences, identifying the classes that really matter to us, no one gives testimony about how much they learned from professors who were disassociated, unable to connect, and self-obsessed. Many charismatic professors are narcissistic yet they may pride themselves on their ability to move through this narcissism to empathize and care about the fate of students both in the class-room and beyond. Like all caring teachers they see that to be successful in the classroom (success being judged as the degree to which we open the space for students to learn, get-ting at that root meaning of the word to educate: to draw out) they must nurture the emotional growth of students indirectly, if not directly. This nurturance, both emotional and academic, is the context where love flourishes.

In our nation most colleges and universities are organized around the principles of dominant culture. This organiza-tional model reinforces hierarchies of power and control. It encourages students to be fear-based, that is to fear teachers and seek to please them. Concurrently, students are encour-aged to doubt themselves, their capacity to know, to think, and to act. Learned helplessness is necessary for the maintenance of dominator culture. Progressive teachers see this helpless-ness in students who become upset when confronting alterna-tive modes of teaching that require them to be active rather than passive. Student resistance to forms of learning that are not based on rote memory or predictable assignments has almost become a norm because of the fixation on degrees rather than education. These students want to know exactly what they must do to acquire the best grade. They are not interested in learning. But the student who longs to know, who has awakened a passion for knowledge is eager to experience the mutual communion with teacher and subject that makes for profound engagement.

Competition in the classroom disrupts connection, making closeness between teacher and students impossible. Just as the insistence on objectivism negates community, the emphasis on competition furthers the sense that students stand in an adver-sarial relationship to themselves and their teachers. The pre-dation that is at the heart of dominator culture emerges when students feel they must symbolically destroy one another in order to prove that they are the smartest. Even though students enter universities at similar levels of capability and skill, it is not assumed that the classroom will be a communal place where those skills will naturally lead to overall excellence on the part of all students. Competition rooted in dehumanizing practices of shaming, of sado-masochistic rituals of power, preclude communalism and stand in the way of community. If students enter a class all sharing similar skills and capabilities and thus common bonds, strategies of distancing and separation must be deployed to effectively disrupt these organic ties. Rather than regarding each other as comrades, students are taught to see each other as adversaries struggling to compete for the prize of being the one smart enough to dominate the others.

Dominator culture promotes a calculated objectivism that is dehumanizing. Alternatively, a mutual partnership model invites an engagement of the self that humanizes, that makes love possible. I began to think about the relationship between struggles to end domination and love in an effort to understand the elements that made for successful movements for social justice in our nation. Looking at anti-racist civil rights struggle, one of the most revolutionary movements for social justice in the world, it was clear that the focus on a love ethic was a central factor in the movement's success. In *All About Love: New Visions* I defined love as a combination of care, commitment, knowledge, responsibility, respect, and trust. All these factors work interdependently. They are a core foundation of love irrespective of the relational context. Even though there is a difference between romantic love and the love between teacher and pupil, these core aspects must be present for love to be love.

When these basic principles of love form the basis of teacher-pupil interaction the mutual pursuit of knowledge creates the conditions for optimal learning. Teachers, then, are learning while teaching, and students are learning and sharing knowledge. In *To Know as We Are Known* Parker Palmer contends that "the origin of knowledge is love," declaring: "The goal of a knowledge arising from life is the reunification and reconstruction of broken selves and worlds. A knowledge of compassion aims not at exploiting and manipulating creation but at reconciling the world to itself. The mind motivated by compassion reaches out to know as the heart reaches out to love. Here, the act of knowing is an act of love, the act of entering and embracing the reality of the other, of allowing the other to enter and embrace our own. In such knowing we know and are known as members of one community . . ." This is the spirit of communalism competition works to disrupt and destroy.

The culture of fear that is rampant on most college campuses, present in and outside the classroom, undermines the capacity of students to learn. Fear-based students doubt that they can accomplish what they need to accomplish. More often than not they are overwhelmed by fear of failure. When students are encouraged to trust in their capacity to learn they can meet difficult challenges with a spirit of resilience and competence. Teaching at a Methodist liberal arts college where professors and administrators affirmed, to greater or lesser degrees, the need for diversity and appreciation for difference on campus, I was struck by the fact that no one wanted to deal with the reality that most students were coming from homes where religious teachings had encouraged them to fear difference, to exclude rather than include voices and perspectives different from their own, to shun diversity. Attending college and being suddenly presented with a different worldview placed them in an adversarial relationship with the family values and spiritual beliefs they had learned. When no recognition and care is given the inner conflicts they face, students in these circumstances may either ruthlessly uphold the status quo (that is, cling to the way things have always been—repudiating engagement with diversity) or fall into debilitating states of apathy and depression. To avoid stress and conflict they simply shut down. Teachers who extend the care and respect that is a component of love make it possible for students to address their fears openly and to receive affirmation and support.

Contrary to the notion that love in the classroom makes teachers less objective, when we teach with love we are better able to respond to the unique concerns of individual students while simultaneously integrating those of the classroom community. When teachers work to affirm the emotional well-being of students we are doing the work of love. Colleagues have shared with me that they do not want to be placed in the role of "therapist"; they do not want to respond to emotional feeling in the classroom. Refusing to make a place for emotional feelings in the classroom does not change the reality that their presence overdetermines the conditions where learning can occur. Teachers are not therapists. However, there are times when conscious teaching—teaching with love—brings us the insight that we will not be able to have a meaningful experience in the classroom without reading the emotional climate of our students and attending to it. In some cases that may require becoming more emotionally aware of psychological conflicts within a student blocking the student's capacity to learn. It may then be appropriate to steer a student in the direction of therapeutic care.

Sometimes professors are fearful of engaging students with love because they worry about being engulfed. They worry they will become too enmeshed in a student's dilemmas. This fear is keenly felt by anyone who is unable to establish appropriate boundaries. Most of us have been raised with a misguided understanding of love. We have been taught that love makes us crazy, makes us blind and foolish, that it renders us unable to set healthy boundaries. Teaching with love, at the end of the semester I had students in my office complaining because they did not receive the grade that they thought they would have received. After all, I cared about them. Their sense of my love/care was that it would lead me to give them higher grades than they deserved. I had this experience several times. Finally, I openly discussed at the start of each new class that there would be no correlation between my loving a student and the student's grade, that the grade would be solely determined by the quality of the work. I explained to the students that, rather than blinding me to the true nature of their abilities, love for them was far more likely to enhance my understanding of their capabilities as well as their limitations, helping them embrace a new understanding of the true meaning and value of love.

When as teachers we teach with love, combining care, commitment, knowledge, responsibility, respect, and trust, we are often able to enter the classroom and go straight to the heart of the matter. That means having the clarity to know what to do on any given day to create the best climate for learning. Teachers who are wedded to using the same teaching style every day, who fear any digression from the concrete lesson plan, miss the opportunity for full engagement in the learning process. They are far more likely to have an orderly classroom where students obey authority. They are far more likely to feel satisfied because they have presented all the information that they wanted to cover. And yet they are missing the most powerful experience we can offer students, which is the opportunity to be fully and compassionately engaged with learning.

Often teachers want to ignore emotional feeling in the classroom because they fear the conflict that may arise. Much as everyone likes to imagine that the college campus is a place without censorship, where free speech prevails and students are encouraged to engage in debate and dialectical exchange, the opposite reality is a more accurate portrait of what takes place in college classrooms. More often than not students are afraid to talk for fear they will alienate teachers and students. They are usually terrified of disagreeing if they think it will lead to conflict. Even though none of us would ever imagine that we could have a romantic relationship with someone where there is never any conflict, students and sometimes teachers, especially in the diverse classroom, tend to see the presence of conflict as threatening to the continuance of critical exchange and as an indication that community is not possible when there is difference.

Many of us have not witnessed critical exchanges in our families of origin where different viewpoints are expressed and conflicts resolved constructively. Instead, we bring to classroom settings our unresolved fears and anxieties. The loving classroom is one in which students are taught, both by the presence and practice of the teacher, that critical exchange can take place without diminishing anyone's spirit, that conflict can be resolved constructively. This will not necessarily be a simple process.

When I taught a seminar on the work of African-American novelist and essayist James Baldwin I just assumed that students signing up for the class would be aware that he was homosexual and want to know more about the ways this experience informed his work. Teaching at a state school, in a classroom that was predominately non-white, initially I was not prepared to cope with a class where some students were shocked to learn that Baldwin was gay and expressed openly homophobic remarks. These students also assumed that they could say anything since gayness was "out there" and not "in here" with us. Their heterosexist thinking prevented them from even considering that gay students might be taking this class. From the moment class began I had to work with loving kindness at establishing a learning community, in a context where the expression of different viewpoints was potentially a threat to the well-being of gays and non-homophobic straight students. By openly talking about the context of love in community, we had to talk about the place of judiciously withholding a viewpoint if it was damaging to others in the community. We had to confront the difference between hate speech and simply stating an opinion. Students who were freaked out by learning that Baldwin was gay also had to learn that we were not an audience for their freaked-out-ness.

Our group became a learning community because we privileged respect and responsibility as needed values in a context where one person's viewpoint could damage the self-esteem and well-being of someone else. Students had to learn the difference between "trashing" someone or a subject and offering careful critique. This classroom was charged with emotional feeling, with painful feelings. Had I ignored their presence and acted as though an objectivist standpoint would create order, the class would have been a deadening experience; students would have *read* Baldwin, but not understood the meaning and significance of his work. Through their work at making community, at creating love in the classroom they could hear more intimately Baldwin's declaration of love's power: "Love takes off the masks that we fear we cannot live without and know we cannot live within. I use the word 'love' here not merely in the personal sense but as a state of being, or a state of grace—not in the infantile American sense of being made happy but in the tough and universal sense of quest and daring and growth." I wish that I could testify that every homophobic individual who took this class underwent a conversion experience and let their hatred go. I cannot. But I can testify that they learned to think beyond the petty boundaries of that hatred. And therein lies the promise of change.

All meaningful love relations empower each person engaged in the mutual practice of partnership. Between teacher and student love makes recognition possible; it offers a place where the intersection of academic striving meets the overall striving to be psychologically whole. While I approach every teaching experience with a general spirit of love, a relationship of love often flourishes between a particular student and myself, and that abides through time. Students I love most intimately never seem to leave my life. As they grow and become teachers or enter professions, they still call on me to teach, guide, and direct them. That our teaching relationship formed and shaped by love extends beyond our time in the classroom is an affirmation of love's power. When I asked one of my students, now a law professor, if my love of her created a climate of favoritism in the classroom, she laughed stating: "Are you kidding? The more you loved us, the harder we had to work." There can be no love without justice.

Love in the classroom prepares teachers and students to open our minds and hearts. It is the foundation on which every learning community can be created. Teachers need not fear that practicing love in the classroom will lead to favoritism. Love will always move us away from domination in all its forms. Love will always challenge and change us. This is the heart of the matter.

Teach 12

Good Sex

Passionate Pedagogy

When I first went to teach at Oberlin College, a big debate about my sexual preferences took place on the wall of a women's rest room. In constructive, politically correct fashion, those walls were covered in paper. This also allowed me to take the document home and place it among my own papers. This public discussion, which really centered around the question of whether or not I was a lesbian, came to my attention only when it led to actual face-to-face conflicts between white and black female students on campus. A black female student felt it was invasive. Annoyed that white female students were "daring" to have this discussion about a black woman professor, she had written: "Bitch, what's it to you anyway. She don't want you." The comment led white females to confront this student about her sexism; she then challenged them about their racism. The black student felt that, had I been a white female professor, this level of disrespect would not have been shown me. In the many discussions that ensued, both organized and on the grapevine, we talked about why it was so important for students to know my, or any, professor's sexual preference; about the danger of attempting to "out" any untenured professor in a homophobic institution; about whether feminist students think they can do no wrong; and most importantly, we talked about the ways black and white females often think differently about matters of sexuality.

Black females in this society come to womanhood in a culture that has never cared for our sexual well-being. Cast in racist and sexist iconography as sexually licentious at all times, most black females risk encountering some degree of sexual harassment and coercion at an early age. In many ways, black females are cynical. No matter how young or old, most of us know, or learn the hard way, that our true stories of rape and sexual harassment tend either not to be believed or deemed unworthy of serious attention, especially if the culprit is someone close, a family member, a boyfriend, or just the man next door.

Given the lack of concern for our sexual well-being, many black females learn that we can best be safe by acting responsibly or that we can best survive victimization by acknowledging some degree of accountability if we have colluded in any way to create a context where we are assaulted. A vast majority of black females seek to protect themselves, their bodies, from random assault by simply closing down sexually, by giving off fierce anti-sex, puritanical, "don't-come-anywhere-near-me-or-I-will-kill-you" vibes. These black women are among that group most likely to take the side of the man in any case of sexual violence against another woman they perceive as not having protected herself. Hence, the black women who had no respect for what they took to be Anita Hill's whining, or Desiree Washington's complaining that Mike Tyson raped her. Their voices were among those saying "What was she doing going to his room in the wee hours of the morning anyhow? She was asking for trouble. In the eyes of black women who expect black females to get a grip and know the score, to ask for trouble and not to know how to handle it is to be complicit. The score means that nobody cares about the black female body— she must do the caring if she wants to be safe. A major emphasis then in black female life is on "prevention" rather than crisis management after victimization. In the dog-eat-dog world of street survival, victims who have placed themselves at risk by doing something deemed stupid don't get a lot of sympathy. Folks may care for your pain and at the same time give you a harsh "read" for not being on the job, that is to say, not maintaining your own critical awareness about the predatory nature of male-female relations in the context of white-supremacist capitalist patriarchy. Such thinking on the part of many black females has often meant that in diverse black communities sexual assault is not taken seriously enough, while on the other hand many white females in the culture tend to be obsessed with issues of sexual victimization.

In my work I have tried to convey a basic, commonsensical understanding of the myriad ways black females—and all females—must protect ourselves, must assume more responsibility than we should have to assume in a sexist racist world. I have consistently called on women to resist identification with victimhood as the only possible location from which to struggle for social change. As an advocate of revolutionary feminist politics, I oppose all forms of sexual violence against women. At the same times, I see the need for a liberatory context for the assertion of female sexual agency within the existing patriarchal culture as an equally important agenda of feminist movement. To claim one's sexual agency any woman has to believe that she can be responsible to her self and to her body in ways that both enhance her capacity to experience sexual fulfillment and her ability to be protective so as to diminish the likelihood that she will ever be sexually victimized. Those mainstream feminists who have been all too eager to represent women as always and only victims have been more than chastised by a public that is sick of whining, that is bored with pathological narcissism and the utter refusal to acknowledge that we are ever complicit in our victimization. Self-appointed dominatrix divas like Camille Paglia, and her younger version, Katie Roiphe, join the anti-feminist backlash crowd in denouncing all female claims to victimhood, whether real or imagined. The saga continues. Severe media-bashing of those mainstream nouveau-Victorian feminists who see everything, even a harsh word as assault or rape, has done little to intervene on the growing bond between this group and their right-wing sisters and brothers who are equally eager to set the struggle for female sexual agency and women's liberation back a few hundred years.

One of the newest arenas in which assertions of female sexual agency are under attack is the debate over whether erotic relationships between professors and students can ever be appropriate. This debate has emerged only as a significant issue in mainstream culture now that individual female students have filed civil suits against both professors accused of sexual violence and the institutions they work for. The threat of losing these suits and having to pay huge sums of money is leading institutions like Harvard, Tufts, the University of Pennsylvania, and many others to develop policy aimed at regulating and/or prohibiting romance between students and faculty. Yet this attempt at regulation does not emerge from a concern on the part of institutions to "protect" students from sexually licentious professors eager to do them harm. Within all these institutions, women who identify themselves as feminists have for years worked hard to institutionalize policy that would more aggressively challenge and punish those professors, primarily men, who use sexuality to coerce and dominate students, who are usually but not always females. These women wholeheartedly throw their support behind conservative institutional efforts to ban faculty/student relationships.

Years ago at the University of California Santa Cruz where I was a graduate student who taught Women's Studies courses, I sat on a committee working on sexual harassment policy. I remember giving a little speech about why prevention and not punishment should be our primary agenda, but no one wanted to listen. The part of the speech that turned everyone off was the suggestion that during orientation of first-year students there might be a space for playful skits that would dramatize situations where professors would make inappropriate overtures toward students, and then actors in the skits pretending to be students would show the best way to handle such situations. I proposed a skit that would simply show a flirtatious male professor inviting a female student to bring her paper over to his house in the late evening so that they could go over it together and her responding that it would be best for them to meet during office hours. When I presented my idea I was met with a complete lack of interest in brainstorming about ways that would empower students to protect themselves against unwarranted advances. This made me aware that many of these women really were more interested in reinforcing the idea that men are always and only sexual oppressors, and that females, especially young adults, are always and only victimized by sexuality. They were not interested in empowering female students, in preventing them from being "hurt;" they wanted to identify and punish perpetrators. Underlying this zeal to punish the "guilty" men was a real discomfort with active sexuality, a refusal to recognize female students as young adults capable of asserting sexual agency. Their need to deny that female students ever attempted to entice and seduce professors, thereby making the issue not always simply one of desire on the professor's part, was so intense as to be mind-boggling. As the meeting progressed it became clear that the issue was not preventing professors from using sexuality to coerce or dominate, but rather a disapproval of all erotically based relations between professors and students. If these women could have institutionalized policy that would condemn all such relationships they would have. Today, more conservative feminist scholars who think this way are willing to join forces with anti-feminist supporters of patriarchy, in an effort to police desire on college campuses so that all romantic relationships between professors and students will be outlawed, will be seen as the same as those relations where professors use sexuality to coerce and dominate students, especially individuals over whom they exercise power. This includes students who are in their classes, whose committees they serve on, who need recommendations, and so forth. That conservatism can be heard in the insistence on the part of a woman professor at the University of Virginia who supports bans when she asserts: "This is about the abuse of power, not romance." Actually, in some cases it *is* about romance, and in other cases the issue *is* abuse of power.

Many male professors who publicly oppose the attempt to ban all erotic relations between professors and students are often individuals who have been formally or informally accused of abusing their power. They can be as extreme as their opponents, insisting that abuse is not a problem. The truth is more complex. There have always been positive erotic bondings between professors and students, even in the old days, when explicit institutional policies forbidding such relationships existed. And there have always been professors, primarily males, who use sexuality to coerce and dominate individual students whom they exercise power over. While it is important that we name and vigilantly challenge abuses of power wherein the erotic becomes a terrain of exploitation and/or oppression, it is equally important for us to acknowledge the erotic as a site of empowerment and positive transformation. Eroticism, even that which leads to romantic involvement between professors and students, is not inherently destructive. Yet most individuals who oppose consensual romantic bondings between professors and students act as though any surfacing of sexual desire within an institutional hierarchy is necessarily victimization. Such thinking is rooted in the assumption that "desire" is problematic and not the way in which erotic feelings should be expressed. Extreme supporters of such bans represent students as children and professors as parents. They see any erotic bonding between the two as symbolic incest, and therefore necessarily a violation of the student/child. Not surprisingly, students are among those that most oppose such thinking. Students understand clearly whose interests are served when they themselves are infantilized. Professors who are most wedded to conventional hierarchy are those most interested in applying a parental paradigm to professors and students. Ironically, it is often those male professors who are symbolically acting as "parent" who may exploit the trust between themselves and students.

The public debate about faculty-student relationships is falsely constructed as being gender-neutral. In actuality, the individuals who prey on students, the repeat offenders who use their sexuality to coerce and dominate, are almost all men. Neutral terms like "faculty-student relations" actually mask the reality that this is about powerful male professors abusing less powerful students. How many female professors have been accused of raping, sexually coercing, stalking and harassing students? Or of punishing students by ruining their careers for not giving sexual favors? The real political issues obscured in this debate have more to do with the construction of masculinity within patriarchy and the eroticization of domination.

Yet to really confront the issue of male professors abusing students we would need to talk about ways to eradicate patriarchy. It is in patriarchy's interest to make it appear that there is a gender-neutral category of powerful "professor" and a powerless category of "student," and that the moment a relation between two individuals in these categories is eroticized, exploitation and domination are bound to occur. This is a paradigm that makes it seem that neither individual is making choices or has control over their behavior. In a *Time* magazine article, "Romancing the Student," all the identified victims are female and all the professors male. Reporting on a survey conducted by a clinical social worker at the University of Connecticut, Nancy Gibbs asserts: "More than half the male faculty members agreed that a professor who sleeps with a student he supervises is taking advantage of her." They agreed "that a student who breaks up with a professor risks unfair reprisals." Of course much of the data in this survey and in similar studies merely documents that what is true of patriarchy outside the academy is as true inside the academy as well.

If the problems of abuse in faculty/student relations were solely a function of power differences then, as women have gained presence and power in the academy, there should in theory be a huge rise in the number of female professors who are using their power to coerce and dominate students, to engage in acts of sexual violence and harrassment. Cases involving women professors are rare. Why is it easier for everyone, including feminists, to talk about the dangers of exploitation and abuse in erotic relationships between faculty and students, than it is to theorize and talk about why it is some—not all—academic men who abuse their power, often at great risk to their own careers? What is happening in the construction of male sexuality within patriarchy that makes many academic men erotize domination, become sexually obssessed with students, be unable to cope with sexual rejection, or be compulsively addicted to pressuring students into affairs, or in extreme cases committing rape? These problems will not be addressed by more stringent rules and regulations.

Years ago I lived with a male professor who was often approached by female students desiring romance. Our usual response was to talk about the difficulty of knowing the appropriate action to take in such situations. He believed, as I did and do, that it was inappropriate for professors to be involved with students with whom they are working. Weeks before he was coming up for tenure review, he confessed to having a sexual encounter with a female student who had approached him. I was really shocked that he would place his career in jeopardy for the type of sexual encounter that he could have had at any time and had never chosen to have. This student could easily have charged him with sexual harassment—even though she was the one who knocked on our front door with a birthday cake and a suggestive birthday card. When he did not want to continue the encounter, she followed him around, showing up at public events trying to get his attention. He shunned her not because he was no longer attracted to her, but because he realized that he had crossed a line, in part because of his own fears and anxiety about failure, about the possibility of not making it. The issue for him was related to masculinity and work. No doubt this student was hurt by his rejection. She may even have felt that he took advantage of her adoration. This was not a case of abuse, of a lascivious professor erotizing domination. Both these individuals were vulnerable for different reasons. While this encounter was inappropriate, it was obviously generated by a particular set of circumstances that are common on college campuses.

Why is there so little work done about aging men in the academy, who are troubled about the potential loss of sexual allure and potency, yearly facing a new array of students who will remain young for the duration of their stay in our classrooms, many of whom will also be seeking affirmation of their sexual desirability. It is only in the context of an anti-sex culture that the response to the issue of desire between faculty and students would be simply to try and police that desire, rather than to understand it and empower us all to confront it more constructively. Of course that would mean understanding the difference between consensual encounters between faculty and students—which may or may not be problematic—and situations of sexual harassment and coercion.

During my more than twenty years as a faculty member, I have known many individual male professors who preyed upon students. They seemed to be the kind of smart nerdy guys who didn't get pussy in high school and were out to get revenge. Now they pursued every prom queen or cheerleader who pressed that particular adolescent rejection button. When I was an undergraduate at Stanford University, at the peak of a contemporary feminist movement that was really excited about liberating females to assert our sexual agency, this type of professor was usually identified early on and we learned to stay away from them. Hence, his need to prey on new female students who are usually the most uninformed. Like many individual male professors, most of whom are not repeat offenders (by that I mean guys who sexually prey upon students every semester, taking advantage of and/or exploiting students sexually), these guys were sometimes appealing, and quite capable of seducing females without coercion. They seemed to need that power imbalance to be able to get it up and keep it up. Such men's sexual desire is heightened by situations where they wield power over someone who is powerless. They are definitely "into" the erotization of domination.

As undergraduates, we female students would talk about unattractive, nerdy professors who probably had never had any sex appeal in their lives before they became teachers, and who were suddenly seen as sexy by adoring students. Female students in our dormitory loved to joke about our crushes on these guys, and the effort we made to seduce them. We were not eroticizing domination, we were eroticizing power. We fantasized about the pleasure and danger of having sex with a powerful man. This was definitely the stuff of all the romantic novels we had ever read, and we were hot to try the real thing.

Well, I am here to testify—it was usually deeply disappointing. As young female students who fucked professors, we were not seeking to be in a peer relationship. We were, however, convinced that the erotic was a space of growth, and we believed that something about us would be magically transformed by our involvement with "brilliant" men of power. Most of us were terribly disappointed to find that the average male professor did not share that concern, that they were not interested in our self-actualization, they were really in it for the pussy, for the adoration. And even though some meaningful romantic and love relationships emerged between individual male faculty and female students, the vast majority of these men were in fact taking advantage.

Most of us were not damaged by these encounters. Most of us were not abused. But we were hurt. And we learned from these experiences. One awesome lesson was the difference between the eroticization of power and the eroticization of domination. We were fascinated by power. All too often, male professors were only interested in domination. We were trying to understand the meaning of female sexual agency. We were into choice and into pleasure. We loved to chant slogans from feminist novels that urged "This above all else, refuse to be a victim."

When I became a professor I was amazed by the extent to which students, male and female, approached me for romantic and/or sexual encounters. My students seem to desire me much more often than I them. Like many unattached female professors in the academy, I have constantly been the subject of student gossip. Often the students I love the most do the most talking. When I have complained to them about their obsession with my sex life, they have simply responded by telling me to get a grip and accept that it goes with the turf. They want to understand female sexual agency. They want to know how women professors who are sensual and sexual beings cope and work in patriarchal institutions, and how to juggle issues of sexual desirability, agency, and professional careerism. They see us as charting the path they will follow. They want guidelines based on lived experience.

Contemporary feminist movement has usefully interrogated the way powerful men in patriarchal culture often use that power to abuse and sexually coerce females. That necessary critical intervention is undermined when it obscures recognition of the way in which desire can be acknowledged in relationships between individuals where there is unequal yet non-abusive power. It is undermined when any individual who is in a less powerful position is represented as being absolutely without choice, as having no agency to act on their own behalf. As long as young females are socialized to see themselves as incapable of choosing those situations of erotic engagement that would be most constructive for their lives, they will always be more vulnerable to victimization. This does not mean that they will not make mistakes, as I and countless other female students did when we chose to have disappointing non-productive romantic liaisons with professors. The point is that we were not embracing a psychology of female victimization. That would have been utterly disempowering. There is clearly a connection between submitting to abuse and the extent to which any of us already feels that we are destined to be victimized. Academic institutions will do a grave disservice to students, female and male if, via rules and regulations regarding erotic encounters with professors, they construct the student from the onset as a victim.

Any relationship where there is an imbalance of power will be problematic; it need not be a context for exploitation or abuse. The vast majority of women who are heterosexual in this society are likely to be in intimate relations at some point in their lives with men, who have greater status and power. Clearly, it is more important for all of us to learn ways to be "just" in situations where there is a power imbalance, rather than to assume that exploitation and abuse are the "natural" outcome of all such encounters. Notice how conventional binary thinking fixes those in power in ways that deny their accountability and choice by assuming that they can only act on behalf of their interests exclusively. And that their interests will always be antithetical to the interests of those who are less powerful.

Contemporary focus on victimization rarely acknowledges that the erotic is a space of transgression that can undermine politics of domination. Rather than perceiving desire between faculty and students as always and only dangerous, negative and destructive, why not consider the positive uses of that desire, the way the erotic can serve to enhance self-actualization and growth? We hear much more about the way in which individuals have abused power in faculty/students relations where there is erotic engagement; we rarely hear anything about the ways erotic desire between teacher and student enhances individual growth. We do not hear about the affectional bonds that spring from erotic encounters and that challenge conventional notions of appropriate behavior. Most professors, even the guilty ones, would acknowledge that it is highly problematic and usually unproductive to be romantically involved with students they are directly working with, either in the classroom or on a individual basis. Yet, prohibitions, rules, and regulations will not keep these relationships from happening.

The place of vigilance is not in forbidding such encounters but in having a system that effectively prevents harassment and abuse. At every college campus in this country there are individual male professors who repeatedly harass and coerce students to engage in sexual relations. For the most part, even when there have been ongoing complaints, college administrators have not confronted these individuals or used the already institutionalized procedures governing harassment to compel them to stop their abusive behavior. Even though everyone seems to be quite capable of recognizing the difference between those professors who abuse their power and those who may have a consensual romantic relationship with a student, that difference is denied by rules and regulations that affect all faculty and students.

Some folks want to argue there is no difference, that the student is always more vulnerable. It is true that relationships where there are serious power imbalances can be a breeding ground for victimization. They can begin with mutual consent, yet this does not ensure that they may not become conflictual in ways that lead the more powerful party to become coercive or abusive. This is true in all relationships in life. Power must be negotiated. Part of maturing is learning how to cope with conflict. Many exploitation cases involve graduate students and professors. It is difficult to be believe that any graduate student is not fully aware of the risks when she or he becomes erotically involved with a professor who has some control over their career. Concurrently, sexism and misogyny have to be seen as factors at work whenever powerful male professors direct their attention at exceptionally smart female graduate students who could easily become their competitors. If campuses really want to address the problems of abuse in faculty-student relations then we should be socializing undergraduates to be realistic about the problems that can arise in such encounters.

The *Time* magazine story on romantic relations between students and faculty begins with this confession: "During the three months in 1993 when she was sleeping with her English professor, Lisa Topol lost eighteen pounds. She lost interest in her classes at the University of Pennsyslvania, lost her reputation as an honor student and wondered if she was losing her mind. If she tried to break up, she thought, he could ruin her academic career. Then she made some phone calls and learned a bit more about the professor she had come to view as a predator." If one took out the words academic and professor this would read like the troubled narrative of anyone involved with someone on the job who is their supervisor. The problem with this story is not that it does not tell the truth but rather that it tells a partial truth. We have no idea why Lisa Topol entered this relationship. We do not know if it was consensual. We do not know how or why the male involved became abusive. We do know that he did not become abusive simply because he was her professor. The problem here does not lie with faculty-student relations but with this individual male, and the large numbers of men like him, who prey upon females. Patriarchy and male domination condone this abuse. Yet most men and women in the academy, like the society as a whole, are not engaged in activism that would target patriarchy. There are many faculty-student romances that end in friendship, and some that lead to marriage and/or partnership. Obviously, the professors in these relationships are able to conduct themselves in a manner that is not exploitative despite the imbalance of power. There are many more male professors involved with students who are not abusive than those who are.

Realistically, our pedagogy is failing both inside and outside the classroom if students have no awareness of their agency when it comes to choosing a relationship of intimacy with a faculty member. Some folks oppose faculty-student erotic bondings because they say it creates a climate of favoritism that can be deeply disruptive. In actuality, any intimate bonding between a professor and a student contains the potential for favoritism, whether or not that intimacy is erotic. The fact is, there are many situations where favoritism surfaces in the classroom that have nothing to do with the presence of desire. Most professors, for example, are especially partial to students that do assigned work with rigor and intellectual enthusiasm. This is a kind of favoritism, but no one is seeking to either eliminate, question, or police it.

Young females and males entering college are in the process of claiming and asserting adult status. Sexuality is as much a site where that evolution and maturation is registered as is the classroom. Relations between faculty and students, whether merely friendly or erotic, are interactions that should always empower students to be more fully adult.

A college environment should strengthen a student's ability to make responsible mature decisions and choices. Those faculty members who become involved in romantic relationships with a student (whether they initiated it or responded to an overture by the student), who are not exploitative or dominating, will nurture this maturation process. In my teaching career I have had a relationship with one student. I was a non-tenured faculty member at Yale University when this relationship began. Although, he was a student in my class, I did not approach him during the time that he studied with me because I did not want to bring that dynamic either into the classroom or into my evaluation of his work. He was not an exceptional student in my class. When the course ended, we began to be intimate.

From the start we had conflicts about power. The relationship did not work, yet we became friends. Recently, he was visiting me and I shared that I was writing this piece. I wanted to know if he thought I had taken advantage of him. He reminded me of how shocked he was that I desired him because he primarily thought of me as this teacher that he admired and looked up to. In conversation he shared his perspective: "I did not feel in any way coerced. I was just surprised and shocked. I found it intriguing that I would be able to talk to you one-on-one about issues raised in the class. I was happy to have a chance to get to know you better because I knew you were this smart and gifted professor. We all thought you were special. I was young and inexperienced and even though it was exciting that you desired me, it was also frightening." Our romance failed. We had more than our share of miserable conflictual moments; however, our friendship has deepened over the years and is grounded in mutual respect and care.

Student devotion to a teacher can easily be a context where erotic longings emerge. Passionate pedagogy in any setting is likely to spark erotic energy. It cannot be policed or outlawed. This erotic energy can be used in constructive ways both in individual relationships and in the classroom setting. Just as it is important that we be vigilant in challenging abuses of power where the erotic becomes a terrain of exploitation, it is equally important to recognize that space where erotic interaction is enabling and positively transforming. Desire in the context of relations where hierarchy and unequal power separate individuals is always potentially disruptive and simultaneously potentially transformative. Desire can be the democratic equalizing force—the fierce reminder of the limitations of hierarchy and status as much as it can be a context for abuse and exploitation.

The erotic is always present—always with us. When we deny that erotic feelings will *always* emerge between teachers and students, we preclude the recognition of accountability and responsibility. The implications of entering intimate relations where there is an imbalance of power cannot be understood, or those relations handled with care in a cultural context where desire that disrupts is seen as so taboo that it cannot be spoken, acknowledged, and addressed. Banning relations between faculty and students would create a climate of silence and taboo that would only intensify dynamics of coercion and exploitation. The moment power differences are openly talked about where erotic desire surfaces, a space is created where choice is possible, where accountability can be clearly assessed.

Teach 13

Spirituality in Education

I would like to share what I think about spirituality *in* education and what I do.

Embodying the Teachings

One of the first things I do is bring my body out there with the students: to see them, to be with them.

I never met the Buddhist teacher Chögyam Trungpa Rinpoche, founder of the Naropa Institute, because I was afraid of him. Part of what I was afraid of was what he might move in my body—what he might move in my being. His teachings through his written work, however, have molded who I am as a teacher.

Many of you say to me, "bell, I feel that I know you. I feel that I have been with you as I read your texts." A favorite text of mine, for who I am, is Trungpa Rinpoche's book *Cutting through Spiritual Materialism.* That text constantly pushes me: it gets me to think about what it means to have a life in the spirit. We can't begin to talk about spirituality in education until we talk about what it means to have a life in the spirit. So we are not just teachers when we enter our classrooms, but are teachers in every moment of our lives.

What is charming to me about the Dalai Lama is the way he uses his body as a teaching for us, the spontaneous moment. An important thing for me about Trungpa Rinpoche is the sense of unexpectedness, spontaneity, and mystery that comes through his writing.

To live a life in the spirit, to be true to a life of the spirit, we have to be willing to be called on—often in ways that we may not like.

Calling the Spirit

Trungpa Rinpoche's teachings kept calling me; but I kept saying to myself, "No, I'm not ready for this. It's too much."

Once I was invited to participate in a conference with the Dalai Lama in Boulder, Colorado. I keep teasing people that I was an afterthought. The coordinator in turn teased me, saying that he called seventeen states searching for me. If we want to have intimacy with otherness, sometimes we have to search for it. We may have to search for it in seventeen different states.

The conference was to take place at the time of year when I normally take silence. I don't go anywhere. The conference, however, kept coming to me in myriad ways—but I kept thinking, "I don't want to do this. This isn't where I am right now." But the spirit kept on calling me.

Then I started to get sick. As I was coughing up blood. I kept calling the conference organizer to say, "Sorry, I can't come." But no one answered the phone or called me back. So then I thought, I'll be really slick. I'll call my sister, who was supposed to travel there with me, and I'll tell her, "I'm so sick. Do you *really* want to do this?"

But she said, "Oh, yeah, I really want to go. And I've been needing a break."

That's how the spirit calls sometimes. But we must not pretend, make it seem like living a life in the spirit is easy. On the contrary: living the life of the spirit is difficult. It is not a life that is about how much people are going to like you.

We all act like we "like" the Dalai Lama so much, like we're so delighted by him. But often, when we meet a teacher who plunges us into deep and profound mystery, we don't like it. It's not easy; and it's not easy to be such a teacher.

Opportunity

During the conference we missed a powerful teaching moment. As we sang "Down by the Riverside," the Dalai Lama said that he did not understand what we were singing about. But we did not seize the opportunity to enter that moment, to share with him that connection between the oppression of African and African-American peoples, the continuum that links us to Tibet.

I'm often asked, "Why Buddhism?" "Why would you be interested in Tibet?" Particularly by black people who say, "What about the work here?" "What about all those white Buddhists who don't give a shit about what's happening to us right here?"

I think it is very important not to give away Tibet, but to link the freedom of Tibet with our freedom, and for me to understand, as an African-American woman, that my being is connected to the being of all those toiling and suffering Tibetan people, to know that though I may never see or know them, we are connected in our suffering. That connection is part of our understanding of compassion: that it is expansive, that it moves in a continuum.

I said to my sister about the Dalai Lama: "Gosh, doesn't he look like our brother?" And then I said about two monks sitting there: "Gosh, if they took off those robes, they'd just look like two black people we've known all our lives."

And to what extent would people be delighted by them if they were just black people in some regular old clothing, walking around regular old Boulder? To what extent might we feel fear? Or not seize the opportunity to have some intimacy with otherness?

Liberation of the Spirit

As a girl, touched by the mystical dimensions of Christian faith, I felt the presence of the Beloved in my heart: the oneness of our life. At that time, when I had not yet learned the right language, I knew only that despite the troubles of my world, the suffering I witnessed around and within me, there was always available a spiritual force that could lift me higher, that could give me moments of transcendent bliss wherein I could surrender all thought of the world and know profound peace.

Early on, my heart had been touched by its delight. I knew its rapture. Early on, I made a commitment to be a seeker on the path: a seeker after truth. I was determined to live a life in the spirit.

The black theologian James Cone says that our survival and liberation depend upon our recognition of the truth when it is spoken and lived:

> If we cannot recognize the truth, then it cannot liberate us from untruth. To know the truth is to prepare for it; for it is not mainly reflection and theory. Truth is divine action entering our lives and creating the human action of liberation.

In reflecting on my youth, I emphasize the mystical dimension of the Christian faith because it was that aspect of religious experience that I found to be truly liberatory. The more fundamental religious beliefs that were taught to me urging blind obedience to authority and acceptance of oppressive hierarchies—these didn't move me.

No, it was those mystical experiences that enabled me to understand and recognize the realm of being in a spiritual experience that transcends both authority and law.

Returning Home

As a student in graduate school seeking spirituality in education, I wanted there to be a place in my life for theory and politics, as well as spiritual practice. My quest was to find for them a meeting place.

It is interesting to me that the two spiritual teachers that have been so meaningful to me, and run like threads through my work, are so different in their own beings: Trungpa Rinpoche and Thich Nhat Hanh, the Vietnamese Zen master. Their visions are different in many ways. One so committed to the magic and mystery, the courageous. The other slightly more doctrinaire, but so committed to the notion of openheartedness.

One of the first books that led me down Thich Nhat Hanh's path was a book that he wrote with Daniel Berrigan called *The Raft Is Not the Shore.* In that book, Thich Nhat Hanh writes of self-recovery. In the Buddhist tradition, he says, people used to speak of enlightenment as a kind of returning home.

"The three worlds," he says, "the world of form, of nonform, of desire, are not your homes." These are places you wander off to, the many existences alienated from your own true nature. So enlightenment is the way to get back: the way home.

Thich Nhat Hanh speaks of the efforts to go back in terms of the recovery of one's self, of one's integrity. I began to use this vision of spiritual self-recovery in relationship to the political self-recovery of colonized and oppressed peoples. I did this to see the points of convergence between the effort to live in the spirit and the effort of oppressed peoples to renew their spirits—to find themselves again in suffering and in resistance.

Here is my concern: What is the place of love in this recovery? What is the place of love in the experience of intimate otherness?

When I come here, or to any place and feel myself to be somehow not fully present or seen, what allows me to enter this space of otherness is love. It is the love that I can generate within myself, as a light and send out, beam out, that can touch people. Love can bridge the sense of otherness. It takes practice to be vigilant, to beam that love out. It takes work.

I am awed by all these people who teach at places where spirituality is accepted. Most of my teaching experience has been in climates that are totally, utterly, and completely hostile to spirituality. Where colleagues laugh at you if they think that you have some notion of spiritual life.

So much of my experience, my teaching practice has been honed in that particuarly harsh kind of environment; being spiritual-in-eduation within an environment that is utterly hostile to that. Not naming that hostility but working with it in such a way that the spirit can be present in the midst of it: that the fire burns bright without any generation, anything in the environment generating it.

Howard Thurman maintained that the experience of redemptive love was essential for individual and collective self-actualization. Such a love affirms. In *The Growing Edge*, he contends that whether we are a good person or a bad person, we are being dealt with at the point beyond all that is limiting and all that is creative within us. We are dealt with at the core of our being; and at that core, we are touched and released.

In much of his work. Thurman cautions those of us who are concerned with radical social change to not allow our visions to conform to a pattern we seek to impose but rather allow them to be "modeled and shaped in accordance to the innermost transformation that is going on in our spirits."

To be guided by love is to live in community with all life. However, a culture of domination, like ours, does not strive to teach us how to live in community. As a consequence, learning to live in community must be a core practice for all of us who desire spirituality in education.

All too often we think of community in terms of being with folks like ourselves: the same class, same race, same ethnicity, same social standing and the like. All of us evoke vague notions of community and compassion, yet how many of us compassionately went out to find an intimate other, to bring them here with us today? So that when we looked around, we wouldn't just find a similar kind of class, a similar group of people, people like ourseves: a certain kind of exclusivity.

I think we need to be wary: we need to work against the danger of evoking something that we don't challenge ourselves to actually practice. A lot of white folks can travel all the way to Tibet to experience intimate otherness, but can't imagine the idea of finding an other in their life right where they are, and saying, "Would you like to come with me?"

There was a young woman who said to me at a conference: "I'd like to come tonight, but I didn't register." And I said to her: "Well, here. Just take my little ticket, and you can come on in." I did this just as I was trying to decide for myself, for my day, the answer to the question "What are the actions I will concretely do today in order to bring myself into greater community? With that which is not here?"

I address these concerns by writing to a spiritual comrade, Cornel West, with whom I once had deep, passionate arguments about the meaning of spiritual life, and about what we were called upon to do as educators. One of the things that we argued about was the notion of sacrifical love.

There is that moment of delay that allows us—in the midst of physical suffering and pain—to remember that we are more than our pain. And that there are other ways that we can speak.

One of the things that I constantly hear Thick Nhat Hanh saying in my head is this: "When we are in the midst of the teacher, the teacher does not have to necessarily talk to us." That the presence of their body, their being itself, means something to us. Returning to the concrete.

Perhaps one of the most intense political struggles we face—and greatest spiritual struggle—in seeking to transform society is the effort to maintain integrity of being. In my letter to Cornel, I wrote:

> We bear witness not just with our intellectual work but with ourselves, our lives. Surely the crisis of these times demands that we give our all. Remember the song which asked "Is your altar of sacrifice late?" To me, this "all" includes our habits of being, the way we live. It is both political practice and spiritual sacrament, a life of resistence. How can we speak of change, of hope, and love if we court death? All of the work we do, no matter how brilliant or revolutionary in thought or action, loses power and meaning if we lack integrity of being.

I can testify to the meaningfulness of spiritual practice and that such a practice sustains and nurtures progressive teaching, progressive politics, and enhances the struggle for liberation.

Teach 14

This Is Our Life

Teaching toward Death

Watching my father's mother Rachel die as a child, seeing her there one moment and then gone forever provided me with an early understanding that death could take us unawares. Then there was my mother constantly telling us that "life was not promised"—her admonition that challenged us to move from idleness to action, from indifference to passionate engagement. It has been part of my destiny to contemplate the meaning of death. In my spiritual practice I often focus on meditations meant to strengthen our awareness of death's constant presence, to help us live fully in the moment that we have, the living moment—the present. Ram Dass uses a simple phrase to call us back to the living moment: "Be Here Now."

College education is so often geared toward the future, the perceived rewards that the imagined future will bring that it is difficult to teach students that the present is a place of meaning. In modern schooling the messages students receive is that everything that they learn in the classroom is mere raw material for something that they will produce later on in life. This displacement of meaning into the future makes it impossible for students to fully immerse themselves in the art of learning and to experience that immersion as a complete, satisfying moment of fulfillment.

College as it is envisioned by mainstream culture is seen as a stop on a journey with an endpoint that is always somewhere else. College demands delayed gratification. This is a primary reason many students are chronically disgruntled, frustrated, and full of complaint. Contrary to Ram Dass's call that we "be here now" students are socialized via conventional pedagogy to believe that their own "now" is always inadequate and lacking. One of the few experiences teachers share today irrespective of our political beliefs, standpoint, or disciplines is a general sense of weariness that emerges as we confront this chronic dissatisfaction among students.

The vision of progress that is central to imperialist white-supremacist capitalist patriarchy is one that always places emphasis on the future—there is always a better moment than the moment that is, a better job, a better house, a better relationship. Education as we conventionally know it plays a crucial role as the location where students learn to embrace the values that go with the status quo. Every professor in the humanities has stories to tell about students devaluing what we do, what they learn in our classrooms because they are unable to attach any substantive meaning to experiences that do not directly intersect with their future visions of success. There has probably never been a time in the history of college education where there were classrooms without opportunistic future-oriented students; however, there were times when such students were in the minority. Once upon a time, there were students (and here I include myself) who wanted to stay in college forever because our courses provided an experience of studying, learning, and communal fellowship in the quest for knowledge that was simply divine. Nowadays our classrooms are more likely to be composed of students who are fixated on the main chance, the opportunity they see opening up in the future. Of course these students are obsessed with grades and willing to do almost anything to ensure that they will get the evaluation that most boosts their future chances of success.

As teachers we join them in this fixation on the future when we work for promotion, tenure, good evaluations. Academically, intellectually, much of the work we do invites us to engage in constant analytical processing. More often than not our thinking is aimed in the direction of the past or the future (especially as we work with ideas trying to discover original thoughts that will set us apart from our peers and advance our careers). This mode of thinking can be incredibly fruitful, but unless we can combine it with more passive forms, what Richard Carson and Joseph Bailey call "the free flowing mode," it can deaden our capacity to be in touch with the present. Carson and Bailey stress that when we are engaged solely in analytical thinking we are choosing the relationship to ideas that is most valued in conventional pedagogy. Explaining further they contend: "if you are actively thinking, you are in processing mode; if you are passively thinking, you are in the free flowing mode. When you are in the flow, it feels as if you are not thinking at all. The thinking seems to happen to you. Free-flowing mode thinking moves naturally, constantly bringing you fresh, harmonious, thoughts. When you are in the processing mode, however, the thinking is originating from your memory." When I was in graduate school years ago, the classes wherein I truly learned were those where these two approaches were combined. Yet today's frantic need to push toward deadlines, covering set amounts of material, allows very little room, if any, for silence, for free-flowing work. Most of us teach and are taught that it is only the future that really matters.

This shift in attitude is directly related to our cultural shift from a moment where non-materialist, non-market values co-exist along with the desire to succeed economically to a culture where hedonistic materialism and unchecked consumption is the norm. In a culture "you are what you buy" sonnets can have little meaning. Poetry matters only if it can be used to make a catchy jingle for a commercial, unless they can be used to sell something.

I am among that baby boomer generation of professors who initially entered an academic climate where we expected to work hard and be poorly paid for a lifetime. For many of us the trade-off was that we would have time. We would have long vacations and summers off to think, to write, to dream. Had anyone told me in my twenties that I would one day be paid (for however short a time) a six-figure salary to work as a professor I would have laughed at them. It seemed impossible. And yet I did arrive at the pinnacle of academic success, was offered and accepted a Distinguished Professorship, and was paid that huge salary. I resigned this job relatively soon because I was simply no longer satisfied with myself in the classroom and with the educational climate in the university.

It was difficult to tell the world I was resigning because I knew it would be difficult to explain that I felt I was just not performing with the degree of grace and excellence as a teacher that was the standard by which I judged myself. One of my best friends and academic colleagues tried to convince me that a C+ day in my classroom was like an A+ in other classes at our school. When I announced my plan first to take an unpaid leave for several years and then resign, the feedback I received was that I was crazy. My peers shared their sense that to have been a low-paid professor for more than twenty years who finally gets the big bucks and walk away from it was madness. Their focus was solely on financial reward—the big bucks. They were not particularly concerned with the quality of life in the classroom.

During the two years that I spent on unpaid leave, two more intellectual comrades, writers, and artists were added to the list of the colleagues in my life who have died in the past ten years. Felix Gonzales-Torres, Marlon Riggs, Essex Hemphill, and Toni Bambara. Critic Toni Cade Bambara, the cancer eating away at her life force, scolded me from her hospice bed about my working too hard. This stellar party girl was telling me I needed to party more. Here I was telling her that I did not think I would be throwing big parties, but I would heed the call to take in my environment, to look and live and find or create the spaces of joy.

One of the most memorable classes I ever taught was at Yale. It was a course on African-American women writers. We were reading Toni Bambara's intense book *The Salteaters*. Students accustomed to reading "easy" stories by black women, were struggling. There were more than fifty students in my class. When I called Toni and asked her if she would come and talk with them about her writing, her work, her life choices, she came. A little money changed hands coming from pockets and the department. There was no fame—no public moment in the spotlight—no posters. She mesmerized the students allowing them to hear the firsthand accounts of a writer's process. The conversation between Toni and me added another riff on the book; it was like a moment of jazz improvisation. Students did not want to leave. We just did not want that moment to end. It was one of those moments where everyone was fully present in the now.

These days, such moments rarely happen in a world where most writers want—often desperately—to be paid to come and talk to a class. For years now I have been troubled by the reality that almost all our nation's writers end up working in the academy in order to survive economically. I am troubled because our institutions are conservative and they confine our voices and our imaginations more than we know. Unwittingly, we become our own gatekeepers, representatives of an institution, and not devotees to the sacred world of the imagination. We censor ourselves. We bring an aura of death into the classroom when we close down the imagination's right to say and to do what it needs.

One of the other great teaching and learning moments for me happened when I discovered that Ann Petry, author of the amazing protest novel *The Street*, was living only a few towns away from Yale. I found her number in the phone book and called, not sharing that I had thought her dead because the academy that I lived and worked within did not remember her rightly at the time. After visiting with her in her home and proving to her my love of her work, she journeyed with me to my class at Yale. Short, stout (as my Big Mama would call it), graying (as my Big Mama would think it only proper that an old lady be—gray and proud), she began her talk with a provocative statement about death. This little old lady told us in a voice as sharp and keen as galvanized steel that she knew before she had written a word that Lutie would kill her lover Boots as an act of self-defense.

The grace and sweep of Petry's imagination awed her listeners. I was reminded of June Jordan's declaration: "If the acquirement of my self-determination is part of a worldwide, an inevitable, and a righteous movement, then I should become willing and able to embrace more and more of the whole world, without fear, and also without self-sacrifice. This means that as a Black feminist, I cannot be expected to respect what somebody else calls self-love if that concept of self-love requires my suicide to any degree." Ann Petry gave the world one of the first portraits of a black woman engaged in critical resistance, challenging domination as she faced the intersections of race, sex, and class. Petry is now dead. She lived a long and full life. June Jordan is dead. She too lived fully, but not long enough; like so many black women writers, she died in her prime. When black women comrades, writers and artists, have been in the throes of death there has been a reaching out within the spirit of community, so that from their death and dying we can both learn and teach. In his reflections on dying and caring, *Our Greatest Gift,* Jesuit priest Henri Nouwen (whose work teaches me as it did then when he was yet alive) offers this insight: "Caring together is the basis of community life. We don't come together simply to console each other or even to support each other. Important as those things may be, long term community life is directed in other ways. Together we reach out to others. . . . The mystery of this caring together is that it not only asks for community, but also creates it." In a world where the words of black women writers, even our very names are often soon forgotten, it is essential and necessary that we live through writing and teaching the words of our great and good writers, whose voices must no longer be silenced, not even by death.

Any professor who teaches the work of black women writers is struck by the fact that the vast majority of these books will have been written by females who did not live long enough, who died young. Teaching this work, I am called, both in reflections on the past and by our present existence, to contemplate the meaning of dying as I ponder the quality of life in the classroom.

In recent years the loss of friends, comrades, and colleagues has provided many of us with a steady reminder of death's presence. Here in New York on September 11, not far from the falling towers death seemed so close. My small flat, permeated at times with the stench of smoke carrying the taste of death—brutal, senseless, tragic was no longer a haven. It became a place to confront death. In search of death's meaning, I focus in spiritual practice on the Buddish vision of "our appointment with life" which engages me with sutras on impermanence, the reality of now that Vietnamese Buddhist monk Thich Nhat Hanh evokes as "present moment, only moment." He teaches: "Our true home is in the present moment. To live in the present moment is a miracle. The miracle is not to walk on water. Peace is all around us . . . Once we learn to touch this peace we will be healed and transformed. It is not a matter of faith; it is a matter practice. We need only to find ways to bring our body and mind back to the present moment . . . " His simple words about peace challenge me, and teachers like me, at the core of our being, even as we are obsessed with thinking, analyzing, critiquing. The practice of mindfulness has helped me balance my passion for thinking, for processing—this passion that is the catalyst for ecstatic teaching—with a passion for silence, for the present moment.

When I sit to hear this great teacher lecture, when I sit and speak heart-to-heart to him with no audience, I am called to surrender fully—to be in the present moment. His presence, even without words, calls me there. And I take this mindful practice into the classroom, in hopes that students will learn from my example to be fully where we are—to be here now. He explains: "We tend to be alive in the future, not now. We say, 'Wait until I finish school and get my Ph.D. degree, and then I will be really alive . . . ' We are not capable of being alive in the present moment. We tend to postpone being alive to the future, the distant future, we don't know when. Now is not the moment to be alive. We may never be alive at all in our entire life. There, the technique is to be in the present moment, to be aware that we are here and now, and the only moment to be alive is the present moment . . . This is the only moment that is real." We can share this understanding with our students. We can share it in a five-minute lecture. We can help them trust in the present.

Whenever I was frustrated with the stale, unproductive, deadening energy in my classrooms, I could usually shift the mood by threatening to give my "this is our life" lecture. The one that begins with death and dying. It is a small talk about the quality of life in the classroom, a reminder that our time together can be utterly satisfying, complete, a space where we can lose all thought of the future. It makes students uncom-

fortable to talk about death. They want to cling to the obsession with the future because it is the primary way they make
sense of the present. Coming from a background of conventional pedagogy they usually have no way to value learning for
learning. To them learning is goal oriented. It is not valued in
itself but as a means to something else.

Teaching students to be fully present, enjoying the
moment, the Now in the classroom without fearing that this
places the future in jeopardy: that is essential mindfulness
practice for a true teacher. Without a focus on the "Now" we
can do the work of educating in such way that we draw out all
that is exquisite in our classroom, not just now and then, or at
special moments, but always. Teaching mindfulness about the
quality of life in the classroom—that it must be nurturing, life-
sustaining—brings us into greater community within the classroom. It sharpens our awareness; we are better able to respond
to one another and to our subject matter.

In every classroom there are times when teacher and students are "caught" up, are somewhere else. It is as though we
are collectively in a trance. On those days I often ask my students what is going on. Why are we trapped in such "ennui?"
How can we use this moment as a place to be where we are and
learn from the here-and-now. Within a utopian world we would
be able to dismiss class on such days because educating anyone
when they are not present is impossible. Since we cannot leave
we try to work with the reality that we have to produce the
conditions for learning. We work with our absence to become
present.

I have heard Thay teach about engaged Buddhism, and I
have applied many of these ideas to engaged pedagogy. When
we practice learning in such a way that it brings us into closer
connection without ourselves the classroom is transformed.
Thay describes being in touch as being "aware of what is going
on in your body, in your feelings, in our mind." This state
evokes in us an awareness of *interbeing.* When we practice

interbeing in the classroom we are transformed not just by one individual's presence but by our collective presence. Experiencing the world of learning we can make together in community is the ecstatic moment that makes us come and come again to the present, to the now, to the place where we are real.

Teach 15

Spiritual Matters
in the Classroom

I was trained to keep all discussions of religion and spirituality out of the classroom. When I made the long journey to Stanford University from Virginia Street Baptist church, where my soul had first been touched by the mystical dimensions of Christian faith, I knew that Stanford was not a place there would be any discussion of divine spirit. Of course the "Jesus freaks," as they were called, the born-again Christians spread their word openly. They had no knowledge of Christian mysticism. It was my longing to become an intellectual that had led me all the way from Kentucky to California, the first child in my family to go so far away from home to attend college. My fundamentalist Christian parents actually talked about California as Babylon. They feared I would lose touch with a sense of the sacred there; they feared my soul would be tempted by evil, tempted to turn away from God.

Leaving our familiar, Southern ways of living and being to attend college on the West Coast, I was initially plunged into a wilderness of spirit so intense it felt as though I was breaking into bits and pieces and that I would never feel whole again. Contrary to my parents' fears of Babylon, this wilderness moment, this time in the desert turned me toward religion rather than leading me away. I hoped to find in intimacy with divine spirit, a source of clarity that would anchor me as I opened my mind and heart to embrace the many new ideas and habits of being I faced.

I often sat in silent prayer in the Stanford church, that beautiful sanctuary, close to the English department, and sought solace for my spirit. Communing there I prayed that my faith would grow stronger as my mind worked to meet the challenge of being in this elite educational world. It did not take me long to throw off the rigorous Christianity of my growing up, which required that I find a church home and attend service and weekly prayer meeting regularly. Instead I became immersed in the poetry of Islamic mysticism, studying Sufism and then following the Beat poets into Buddhism. During my undergraduate years at Stanford I first learned about "transcendental meditation." It was there that I first met the poet Gary Snyder and heard about the celebrations on his land that included Buddhists and all seekers on the path. I met my first Buddhist nun at Snyder's mountain sanctuary. Sitting in a circle around around a fire I listened to poetry and chanted songs of praise. As I listened to the chanting and heard the ringing of bells, I felt my spirit awaken. To me it seemed only natural that a black person living in our nation, which was slowly turning away from exploitation and oppression based on race, would understand a spirituality based on the premise that "all life is suffering."

Just as I was starting to immerse myself in the study of Buddhist teaching, Martin Luther King had been touched by the peace activism of a then, little known, Vietnamese

Buddhist monk, Thich Nhat Hahn, whom he encountered through the Fellowship of Reconciliation. Bonded in solidarity by their mutual commitment to non-violence, together they understood the transformative power of suffering. While Thay was teaching that "your suffering has the capacity of showing us the path to liberation," King was teaching about "the value of unmerited suffering." Offering personal testimony, King proclaimed: "Recognizing the necessity for suffering, I have tried to make of it a virtue . . . I have lived these last few years with the conviction that unearned suffering is redemptive." Coping with both a profound sense of dislocation and disconnection I turned away from my classmates and professors to find solace in sacred spaces. I turned toward religion to reconnect. I sought a spiritual foundation to sustain my soul.

Writing in her autobiographical essay "Notes of a Barnard Dropout," June Jordan describes her longing to have college be the place that would connect all the fragmented pieces: "Well, I was born in Harlem, and raised in Bedford Stuyvesant. Then, when I was twelve or thirteen, I was sent away to prep school. In other words, I began my life in a completely Black universe, and then for the three years of prep school, found myself completely immersed in a white universe. When I came to Barnard, what I hoped to find, therefore was a connection . . . I hoped that Barnard College would either give me the connection between the apparently unrelated world of white and Black, or that this college would enable me to make that connection for myself." Jordan's hopes were dashed. She found "none of the courses of study, nothing about the teaching, made the connection for me, or facilitated my discovery of a connection." She dropped out. For many smart students from backgrounds that are marginalized by race, class, geography, sexual preference, or some combination, college continues to be a place of disconnection. Throughout my college experience, both during my undergraduate and graduate years, spirituality was the place where the connections were made for me.

And even though there was no talk of spirituality at Stanford, the open doors of the church offered a constant validation of the place of the sacred in education.

Religion and spirituality are not synonymous. Calling for a spiritual revolution in *Ethics for the New Millennium*, His Holiness the Dalai Lama makes useful distinctions between religion and spirituality:

> "Religion I take to be concerned with faith in the claims to salvation of one faith tradition or another, an aspect of which is acceptance of some form of metaphysical or supernatural reality, including perhaps an idea of heaven or nirvana. Connected with this are religious teachings or dogma, ritual, prayer, and so on. Spirituality I take to be concerned with those qualities of the human spirit—such as love and compassion, patience, tolerance, forgiveness, contentment, a sense of responsibility, a sense of harmony—which bring happiness to both self and others. While ritual and prayer, along with the questions of nirvana and salvation, are directly connected to religious faith, these inner qualities need not be, however. There is thus no reason why the individual should not develop them, even to a high degree, without recourse to any religious or metaphysical belief system. This is why I sometimes say that religion is something we can perhaps do without. What we cannot do without are these basic spiritual qualities."

These distinctions are useful for teachers who want to understand how to bring spirituality to teaching and learning without bringing in religion as well.

In the introduction to *The Heart of Learning: Spirituality in Education*, editor Steven Glazer shares the observation that many people fear religion or spirituality in education because "they are afraid of the imposition of identity" and "the indoctrination of particular beliefs." He explains: "Out of this fear of imposition a great tragedy has taken place . . . the wholesale abandonment of the inner world. This fear has allowed us to ignore in our classroom (and lives) the existence of the inner realm, the realm of spiritual formation, of spiritual identity." Certainly, coming from a segregated black world where claiming spiritual identity had been a place of critical resistance, a way to stand against racist dehumanization, I valued spiritual life.

Studying and teaching at elite schools I learned early on that it was only the work of the mind that mattered, that any care of our souls—our spirits—had to take place in private, almost in secret. In his essay "The Grace of Great Things: Reclaiming the Sacred in Knowing, Teaching and Learning," Parker Palmer urges teachers to transform education so that it will honor the needs of the spirit. Telling teachers "to see a transformed way of the being in the world," he gives voice to spiritual yearning: "In the midst of the familiar trappings of education—competition, intellectual combat, obsession with a narrow range of facts, credits, and credentials—what we seek is a way of working illumined by spirit and infused with soul." Like so many working-class kids coming from families where our parents had not attended college, my vision of what this experience would be like was shaped by an old-fashioned understanding of the intellectual as a being who seeks union of mind, body, and spirit, a union of the intellectual as whole person. Even though I rarely found that understanding affirmed in my academic experience, I continued to work toward this vision of wholeness. All that Palmer says resonated within me. He explains that education, teaching, and learning, is about more than gathering information or getting a job: "Education is about healing and wholeness. It is about empowerment, liberation, transcendence, about renewing the vitality of life. It is about finding and claiming ourselves and our place in the world. . . . I want to explore what it might mean to reclaim the sacred at the heart of knowing, teaching, and learning—to reclaim it from an essentially depressive mode of knowing that honors only data, logic, analysis, and a systematic disconnection of self from the world, self from others." Many students come to schools and colleges already feeling a profound sense of disconnection. Schooling that does not honor the needs of the spirit simply intensifies that sense of being lost, of being unable to connect.

Conventional education teaches us that disconnection is organic to being. No wonder then that black students, students of color, and working-class kids of all races often enter schools, especially colleges, with a learned experience of interconnectedness that places them at odds with the world they have entered. No wonder then that so many of these students perform poorly or drop out. They are deeply threatened at the core of their being by the invitation to enter a mind-set where there is no sense of the sacred, where connection is devalued. Glazer argues that we can resolve this issue of disconnection by "establishing sacredness as the ground of learning." Carefully, he explains: "Sacredness is not understood within a particular religious framework but instead as growing out of two basic qualities of our experience: awareness and wholeness. Awareness is a natural, self-manifesting quality: it is our ability to perceive, experience, and know. . . . Wholeness is the inherent, seamless, interdependent quality of the world . . . Wholeness, however, can be cultivated within us by experiencing this nondual quality of the world. Through experiences of awareness and wholeness, we begin to establish the view of the sacred." When as teachers we create a sense of the sacred simply by the way we arrange the classroom, by the manner in which we teach, we affirm to our students that academic brilliance is not enhanced by disconnection. We show that the student who is whole can achieve academic excellence.

Many of our students come to our classrooms believing that real brilliance is revealed by the will to disconnect and disassociate. They see this state as crucial to the maintenance of objectivism. They fear wholeness will lead them to be considered less "brilliant." Popular ideas of what constitutes academic brilliance continue to perpetuate the notion that the critical thinker is unfeeling, is hardhearted. The assumption seems to be that if the heart is closed, the mind will open even wider. In actuality, it is the failure to achieve harmony of mind, body, and spirit that has furthered anti-intellectualism in our culture and made of our schools mere factories.

Education that serves to enhance our students' journey to wholeness stands as a challenge to the existing status quo. Throughout my educational experience, both as a student and during the early years of my teaching as an assistant professor I felt it was crucial that I say nothing about spirituality in the classroom so that I would not in anyway be imposing my concern with spiritual development on my students. During the years that I taught at Yale, I continually saw students—the best and brightest—despair. I saw them drink and drug themselves, attempt suicide, and engage in all manner of mad behavior. Many of these students were students of color. Mostly, they came from a world of economic privilege and status. Yet like their underprivileged counterparts they were all testifying that there was something missing, that there was an emptiness within. When students would ask me how I survived, how I made it without falling apart, I was compelled to give them an honest account of the sustaining power of spirituality in my life.

Honestly naming spirituality as a force strengthening my capacity to resist enabled me to stand within centers of domi-nator culture and courageously offer alternatives. I shared with my students the basis of my hope. In Rachel Naomi Remen's essay "Educating for Mission, Meaning, and Compassion," she speaks about educators as healers who trust in the wholeness of life and in the wholeness of people. She offers this vital insight: "Now, as educators, we cannot heal the shadow of our culture educating people to succeed in society as it is. We must have the courage to educate people to heal this world into what it might become." This is the vision of transformative education. It is education as the practice of freedom.

None of us thinks that education should enforce an inner life but rather that the inner life should not be ignored. When Steven Glazer addressed the question of how teachers can support "the formation of inner spiritual identity without resorting to indoctrination or imposition of ideology," he replied: "The answer is simply to ground education within experience. Examining closely our perceptions, emotions, and beliefs,— our experience—awareness and insight naturally arise. We are already endowed with the qualities of seeing, recognizing, feeling, and knowing. Spiritual identity arises in and of itself from identification with experience rather than submission to a particular set of concepts or beliefs." Significantly Black Studies, Women's Studies, Cultural Studies, all disciplines that promoted a more holistic approach to learning, all disciplines that have placed value on the experiential, have been those disciplines that have most transformed teaching and learning in colleges.

Were it not for these disciplines, professors in other more mainstream programs and departments might never tried to change their teaching so that it did not reinforce imperialist white-supremacist capitalist patriarchy. Contrary to mass media propaganda that falsely misleads the public to believe the lives and works of white men are no longer studied or are marginalized, there has been no intervention that has altered education so that white men and their work is not at the center. Yet there have been crucial shifts in the way people teach and in the material we teach. The success of these shifts, the success of struggles to free education from the grip of dominator culture so that schooling is not simply a factory for turning out new improved dominators, has led to incredible backlash. There would be no need to attack affirmative action had it not been highly successful despite its setbacks and failures. In just a few years affirmative action policies brought more white women (its primary beneficiaries) and more people of color, especially those of us from working-class backgrounds, into the academy.

We made our voices heard. We made our presence felt. And much has changed. Yet the struggle to transform education continues. In particular, we struggle to find a new language of spirit. In *The Outrageous Pursuit of Hope*, theologian Mary Grey explains that we are seeking a "language of connection which respects difference, and is based on a renewed, more modest universalism, without reproducing the old dominant, hegemonic language, suppressing difference, forcing unity where none could coexist with justice." Rightly, we acknowledge that this new language must include a recognition of the connection between soulfulness and our ability to learn.

When we turn our gaze away from all that has not happened, we can see more clearly the enormous changes individuals have made in just a short space of time, the movement from slavery to freedom, from sexism to feminism, from discrimination to greater openness. All these incredible movements for social justice succeeded when they evoked an ethic of love rooted in the embrace of spirit. It is crucial for spiritual nourishment that we all attend to what works even as we understand the need to continue to resist.

Many of the individuals who worked to create communities of diversity are weary. That weariness often emerges as spiritual crisis. It is essential that we build into our teaching vision a place where spirit matters, a place where our spirits can be renewed and our souls restored. We must become as articulate in naming our joys we are in naming our suffering. Thich Nhat Hanh teaches: "When you have suffered you know how to appreciate the elements of paradise that are present. If you dwell only in your suffering, you will miss paradise." To me the classroom continues to be a place where paradise can be realized, a place of passion and possibility, a place where spirit matters, where all that we learn and know leads us into greater connection, into greater understanding of life lived in community.

Teach 16

Practical Wisdom

Coming to academia thinking of myself first and foremost as an artist (a poet, a painter, a writer), I pursued a teaching career as an avocation. My desire was to create art. This was a decision I made in childhood and I looked for the paths that would nurture and sustain this calling. College was the place where I would have time to study, to read, think, and learn, and I attended hoping it would empower me to be a thinking artist. My leaning toward art was directly related to my experience of the power of imagination. It was the imagination that fueled my hope as a young girl in a working-class Southern black home so that I would be able to create an artistic life for myself. The power of the imagination felt prophetic. In Mary Grey's *The Outrageous Pursuit* of *Hope* she explains that "prophetic imagination is outrageous—not merely in dreaming the dream, but in already living out the dream before it has come to pass, and in embodying this dream in concrete action."

Individuals from marginalized groups, whether victimized by dysfunctional families or by political systems of domination, often find their way to freedom by heeding the call of prophetic imaginations.

By dreaming it I came to believe that I could leave the world of racial apartheid, of patriarchal family dysfunction and find my artistic self. I imagined I would find support in the academic world for my soul's quest for freedom and independence of mind and spirit. During my undergraduate years I began to change my orientation. I did not stop artistic pursuits but I discovered that working with ideas was pure ecstasy for me: I embraced the calling to become an intellectual. This choice fit neatly with a teaching career. The heady years of graduate school taught me otherwise. I learned that being an academic was different from being an intellectual. I learned that most academics were not intellectuals and at heart were disdainful of the intellectual life. In the academic world (just like on the outside) intellectuals were depicted as nerds, geeks, anti-social monsters, just one lost argument away from being sociopaths, incapable of communicating with others. The intellectual was depicted as cold, unfeeling, and unable to function in the context of community. And, most significantly, intellectuals were patriarchal men.

These images were disturbing and disheartening. Yet they did not deter me from choosing an intellectual path, from the passionate pursuit of ideas. Working as an academic within institutional structures that are designed to contain ideas, to repress imaginations and indoctrinate the mind, I have consistently felt extremely frustrated. More often than not, the demands of academia were at odds with intellectual life. Just as I was changing my life so that I could commit myself wholeheartedly to working with ideas, I received national recognition as one of the black intellectuals worth noticing. Suddenly, the label "public intellectual" was applied to me. Like the term "black intellectual" this label was not one I felt a need to reject even though neither term defined my sense of self and vocation. No one really seemed to feel a need to define public intellectual, but the implication seemed to be that public intellectuals as distinct from "intellectuals" were not geeks, nerds, or anti-social, borderline sociopaths, because they were capable of appearing in public and communicating with audiences.

In actuality, just as individual black intellectuals on the Left were gaining recognition, we were labeled "public intellectuals" and lumped together with conservative academics who had never before identified themselves as intellectuals. Like most labels, the term public intellectual was really aimed at diminishing the value and significance of intellectual work by that rare individual—an African-American intellectual. In his book *Propaganda and the Public Mind*, Noam Chomsky offers one of the most useful definitions of public intellectuals when he explains that they "are the ones who are acceptable within some mainstream spectrum as presenting ideas, as standing up for values." The values that they represent usually reflect the status quo. They are conservatives or, at best, liberal on most subjects. Certainly, the work I do cannot be encompassed by this definition.

Chomsky defines "dissident intellectuals" as those who are "defenders of freedom." They are critical of the status quo and they dare to make their voices heard on behalf of justice. Early on in my writing I spoke of myself as a dissident voice. That description still seems most accurate. Ironically, being erroneously labeled a public intellectual has momentarily opened doors for me that often close shortly after I enter. But I have been able to bring a spirit of dissidence into locations where radical thought and action are dismissed or even despised. Unlike the dissident intellectuals who Chomsky describes as "cut out of the system because their work was too honest," I was for a time able to make use of the cult of personality and fame that led some institutions to seek my favor. In actuality, I have never had my pick of jobs. And that seems only fitting. My marginal working relationship within academe has been possible in part because of sexism; women thinkers, no matter how radical, are not seen as threatening because we are not taken seriously. Rarely do we have a constituency. Every year I am invited to lecture at colleges and universities across the nation. Usually radical students are the groups spearheading these invitations. Their ability to make a space to hear dissident voices is a location of hope and possibility.

The decision to leave my tenure-track job was in part a response to the constant harassment I received, the psychological assaults that are usually impossible to document. I stayed in the academic world as a tenured professor longer that I wanted to in part to serve as a beacon for students, letting them know that one could succeed without conforming. Colleagues, like my comrade Ron Scapp, urged me to reconsider having no foot in the academic door; they saw that no one was offering me cushy jobs in cushy places, and that this was symptomatic of the treatment dissident thinkers suffer.

In response to this feedback and critical dialogues with Shannon Winnubst, the philosopher and feminist theorist who invited me to speak at Southwestern University, I accepted a position (which she, along with supportive colleagues, helped design) to come and do informal classes. I use the word "informal" because they were open to anyone and grades were not given. When Shannon asked me what were the circumstances that would entice me to teach, I told her that I would like to teach in an open classroom setting where anyone could come (staff and faculty); that I would like to teach teachers concerned with issues of race, gender, class, and religion in their classrooms; and I would dialogue with students. Bringing me to campus was part of an overall effort to diversify. Given my high profile status as a "public intellectual" I was a useful presence for those who wanted to represent the college as becoming more diverse. Professors and students who had really read from the range of my work were amazed that I would come to a predominately all white town in Texas. Some administrators (including the college president) were delighted and welcomed me into the community. Even though that delight began to diminish when my dissident voice and presence expressed a passion for justice and truth, my voice had been heard.

I didn't go to Southwestern because the money offered me was grand. I could have made as much money in just four lectures. It was first and foremost a response to the intellectual dialogue between Shannon and myself. A white woman lesbian professor of philosophy who is passionate about teaching and justice, she was the "seductive" force telling me "come to this campus—so many of us love your work—we need you." After my first lecture at Southwestern I was moved by the way in which the academic job market has meant that many progressive thinkers end up teaching in small towns at colleges that they would not have dreamed of attending as students let alone choose to teach at if there was an abundance of job choices. Just as I felt I was having a "desert" experience when my academic jobs compelled me to live in places not of my heart's choosing, I identified with the individuals who were at this Methodist campus because of circumstance and fate. I emphasize Shannon's role in bringing me to the campus to illustrate the power of one's person action and presence.

When interviewed for this essay I asked her why she felt it was important to bring me to campus. She replied: "Students get so much out of your writing. Bringing you was bringing this huge, great gift to these students." She added: "All the faculty read your work; It was a point of connection between disciplines. You also attracted folks from the community bridging that gap between town and university." I shared Shannon's enthusiasm for bringing a thinker to her campus that in the ordinary scheme of things would not end up working in a small predominantly white Texas town. Having made a commitment in the past ten years to teach in "unlikely" circumstances, to not always be traveling to places where I am greeted by primarily like minded souls, I wanted to talk with folks who do not think as I do. I wanted to work with and join in fellowship with the few black folks there, the people of color who are often isolated and beleaguered because of their minority presence. While there were many students eager to talk to me at Southwestern, the majority of the students there had never heard of or read bell hooks. The same holds true for faculty members.

Shannon says: "I see who these white male and upper-class white people are and I have no more patience. I'm just frustrated. They will not wake up. They are just wallowing in 'whiteness—the whiteness of white supremacy,' and they just do not see it. When you have people who talk about diversity but are unwilling to do anything about it, nothing changes." Yet in the face of frustration she continues to work for change because, she says, "What else is there to do?" We both understand that change is a process. In her essay "White Privilege: Unpacking the Invisible Knapsack," Peggy McIntosh emphasizes: "Disapproving of the systems won't be enough to change them. I was taught that racism could end if white individuals changed their attitudes. But a 'white' skin in the United States opens many doors for whites whether or not we approve of the way dominance has been conferred upon us." Robert Jensen makes it simple in his essay "White Privilege Shapes the U.S." when he unequivocally states:

> "In a white supremacist culture, all white people have privilege whether or not they are overtly racist themselves." With honesty and clarity he explains: "I have struggled to resist that racist training and the racism of my culture. I like to think I have changed, even though I routinely trip over the lingering effects of that internalized racism and the institutional racism around me. But no matter how much I 'fix' myself, one thing never changes—I walk through the world with white privilege. What

does that mean? Perhaps most important, when I seek admission to a university, apply for a job, or hunt for an apartment, I don't look threatening. Almost all of the white people evaluating me for those things look like me—they are white. They see in me a reflection of themselves—and in a racist world, that is an advantage. I smile. I am white. I am one of them. I'm not dangerous. Even when I voice critical opinions, I am cut some slack. After all, I'm white."

It is this understanding of white privilege and its power that informs the consciousness of white people working to end white supremacy and anti-black racism.

Shannon, like other anti-racist white folks, made her commitment to working to end domination in childhood. Growing up in Texas she was acutely aware of racism; it was there in her family. Confronting her sexuality in high school also created greater awareness of group oppression: "Toward the end of my college years I had to deal with sexuality and that brought real surprises—dealing with all the self-hatred—learning what it feels like to be hated because you are different." Now she can state: "Being a lesbian was hard but was easy because I was still white. It's hard to be a woman, hard to be a lesbian but easy to be white." When I asked Shannon what inspired her to move past the fear of difference that so many white folks are "stuck" in, she says: "When I feel fear in myself I am determined to get rid of it." Yet like Jensen, she understands that being anti-racist does not mean she is not welcomed into the perks of white privilege. Shared whiteness can and often does mediate all the other points of separation in an environment where white supremacy is still the underlying point of connection.

Even though Shannon had mixed feelings about teaching at a Methodist college, she knew that "white Christianity was really a part of my background, and it helps me understand where the students are coming from." While Shannon shared many connections, she is not a believer in religion or spiritual practice. When we disagree most vehemently, this is usually the subject. As we worked to define what allows us to create bonds of solidarity and community in spite of our differences of race, sexual preference, and religion, we both see a spirit of radical openness, that willingness to engage in what Thich Nhat Hanh calls that "true dialogue," where "both sides are willing to change." To me the willingness to change and be changed, to remain always open is a defining principle of intellectual life. It is a way of approaching ideas that is at odds with the prevailing academic strategy where one finds a position, defends it, and sticks with it. Shannon's primary hope was that my presence, my teaching would create the space for deep dialogue or, as she puts it, "breaking into the tough stuff." We both feel this goal was fulfilled.

Dean Jim Hunt believed, and continues to believe, that the most important contribution I made to the campus and will make in the future is encouraging students and faculty to think outside the box. Affirming the success of this educational experiment Jim states: "Having you come here with your unique talents for teaching, for dialogue was vital to us. Teachers here want to help students challenge their assumptions, deconstruct them, and then reconstruct them in a different way. This is what you were able to do for us as a community. This is what teaching is about—not just giving information but taking us inside—changing us from the inside out." Like Jim, I am still awed by all the interventions that took place because of this communal effort at sharing knowledge. It was most exciting for me to teach across differences, especially working both in the classroom and individually with staff. All the discussions I had with people of color, staff, and faculty enhanced our understanding of how we can experience a sense of community in academic settings where racism and white supremacy often permeate interactions.

Working with the library staff, who all welcomed me and made a place for my work to be available to students, was one of the most positive experiences. Librarians rarely get to meet with the intellectuals who come to campus. The time I spent at the library, engaging the librarians who are working hard to create a collection that reflects the diversity of books in our nation, was a major intervention—inspiring for both of us. My positive experiences there made it difficult for me to say no when I was asked to serve even in ways I felt were not always the best use of my skills and time.

When President Jake Schrum and Dean Jim Hunt asked me to give the commencement address I agreed, even though at first I resisted; I am not a feel-good speaker and that's what folks want at commencements. But I was persuaded by both these white men that commencement could also be an occasion to generate critical thinking. Jim Hunt recalls: "You told me no and I talked you into it because I believe that anyone who speaks will speak what they believe. Maybe you intuited that what you believe and what you would say might be difficult for folks to hear." Jim challenged me and my concern that we not always talk to and with people who think as we do. I was finally seduced by the idea of talking to groups of people I would not ordinarily talk with. To me the talk I prepared was not particularly militant or in-your-face radical. Before the event, I had alerted my hosts that I would be speaking about death. I asked that Shannon introduce me, thus ensuring that I would not be the only female speaking, or the only radical voice heard.

The day of commencement, it really struck me that I was about to talk to thousands of white people, many of whom were anti-black racists. I felt afraid. When I finished my talk, many of these white folks expressed their displeasure and disdain by booing. Later, they let their rage be known as they lambasted the university for allowing me to speak. While Jim Hunt maintained solidarity with me throughout, always acknowledging that I had raised questions about whether I was the right speaker for the event from the start, other administrators and colleagues distanced themselves from me. I was accused of having made statements I simply had not made. Jim Hunt understood, since he had to cope with much of the fallout. He still believes that the fact that I was introduced as a "feminist thinker" closed many people's minds even before I had spoken. I had been accepted when it was assumed that I was a public intellectual, someone who would, as Chomsky suggests, "present the values and principles and understanding" of the status quo. But that acceptance stopped when I expressed dissident ideas, however mildly. In our critical reflections on this experience both Jim Hunt and I agree that usually when I lecture there is time for dialogue. We both believe that it is necessary for people to have an opportunity to process new paradigms, new ways of thinking. Dialogue with audiences on the subject of race, class, gender, as well as other topics is something that I do exceptionally well. I learned from this experience that I would rather not speak in situations where I am challenging fixed mindsets and when there is no time for dialogue.

To many onlookers this experience was viewed as a failure of efforts at diversity and inclusion. I saw it as a triumph, first and foremost of free speech, which any college must support to be true to its mission. Southwestern states that its core purpose is to engage in "fostering a liberal arts community whose values and action encourage contributions towards the well-being of humanity." Its values and essential goals are "promoting lifelong learning and a passion for intellectual and personal growth, fostering diverse perspectives, being true to one's self and others, respecting the work and dignity of persons, encouraging activism in the pursuit of justice and the common good." These goals are interdependent and cannot be achieved if any part of the whole is forsaken. I have given other commencement talks, but never at a conservative school. I regard my presence as the commencement speaker at this conservative institution as a victory for free speech at a time when many folks in our nation are attempting to silence others, thus betraying the heart of democracy.

I had also been empowered by a world of "white male privilege" to speak to masses of white people who probably have never listened to a black female give a lecture about any subject, let alone a Leftist dissident feminist black intellectual. I was not speaking to the converted. This speaking across the barriers of difference is radical intervention. Even though that world of conservative and liberal white maleness might have chosen me because it really did not understand where I was coming from, and hoped to make use of me as a token symbol of diversity, this wrong intention still created a space for critical intervention and possible transformation. Its aftermath provoked much dialogue and discussion. As one white male student put it: "How many people remember their commencement speaker, who spoke and what they talked about? This commencement, this talk—we will never forget." He was not a radical student who had been in my classes. He had not read my books. And yet he felt moved by my words, moved to think critically, not to passively agree but to think and question. This is what education as the practice of freedom makes possible. It opens the mind. Just as I spoke in my commencement address about the importance of not merely conforming in college but daring to courageously cling to open-mindedness, to critical thinking, my hope was to embody this courage, this radical openness by my presence. That hope was fully realized. Jim Hunt says: "There is not a week that goes by without my thinking of some of the ideas that were raised."

Throughout my teaching career, I have shared with students my belief in the power of prophetic imagination, telling them again and again "that what we cannot imagine we cannot bring into being." Mary Grey echoes these sentiments when she reminds us that as we dream about the future, about creating beloved communities where there is no domination, "what must be takes priority over what is." Clarifying, she states: "The important point is that prophetic imagination, like poetic imagination, is not confined to some private daydream, but is a fully public imagination, belonging to the public domain, inspiring the full range of communities belonging to it to commitment to fuller visions of well-being . . . Prophetic imagination, or prophetic dreaming, keeping visions alive is what stimulates diverse groups into becoming a culture of life, a biophilic, a life-loving culture . . . " Teaching at Southwestern, working with Shannon and all the incredible radically open faculty, students, and staff I want to single out the cafeteria staff who surrounded me with caring supportive community consistently, while reading bell hooks books and sharing their thoughts. This was and is an experiment in teaching that worked. The experiment was not without pitfalls or disappointments. For those of us who were committed to doing the work, it brought us closer, into true community. In *The Different Drum: Community Making and Peace*, M. Scott Peck defines true community as the coming together of "a group of individuals who have learned how to communicate honestly with each other, whose relationships go deeper than their masks of composure, and who have developed some significant commitment to 'rejoice together, mourn together,' and 'to delight in each other' and make the conditions of other's our own." Certainly, sharing laughter is necessary when we dare to enter the dialogues around difference that often evoke in us remembered woundedness or present pain.

Shannon and I agree that our bonds are made stronger by shared humor, ruthless wit, and the laughter that gives us a break from the seriousness of it all. Even though I am always hearing about the "political correctness" that has made everybody uptight, this is not my experience. It may be my very own brand of down-home, funky Southern style that breaks through the rigidities, but one thing I do know: we need to laugh together to make peace, to create and sustain community. In his memoir *Hunting for Hope*, Scott Russell Sanders asks what values must be taught as a "training ground for life in community." I share with him the values he identifies as "the habits of heart and mind essential for creating and maintaining community." They are "generosity and fidelity and mercy, a sympathetic imagination, a deep and abiding concern for others, a delight in nature and human company and all forms of beauty, a passion for justice, a sense of restraint and a sense of humor, a relish for skillful work, a willingness to negotiate differences, a readiness for cooperation and affection." Such a community constantly restores and renews our hope.

Fundamentally the dedicated students at Southwestern, both professors and undergraduates, all learned about joy in struggle, about the connections between theory and practice. We learned that the movement from talk to action is often a perilous journey. Yet like all great adventures, it positively transforms us. We become more fully ourselves at the journey's end—made whole. Parker Palmer speaks of moving through fear as we begin to learn new ideas, new ways of seeing the world, as we confront differences with no need to annhilate them, confessing: "I am fearful. I have fear. But I don't need to be my fear as I speak to you. I can approach you from a different place in me—a place of hope, a place of fellow feeling, of journeying together in a mystery that I know we share." Dominator culture has tried to keep us all afraid, to make us choose safety instead of risk, sameness instead of diversity. Moving through that fear, finding out what connects us, revelling in our differences; this is the process that brings us closer, that gives us a world of shared values, of meaningful community.

Parker Palmer

Alice Walker

Index